(ARUTHUR)

I HOPE YOU ENJOY MY book!
THESE TALES ARE ALL TRUE.

MiKé

Michael J. McCulley

#3JB TWINKLE TOES
THE
CLOWN

Michael J. McCullough

Growing Up Philly

*From Southwest Philadelphia
to the Jersey Shore*

DEDICATION

This book is dedicated to all of those who grew up in Southwest Philadelphia. We lived in a neighborhood much like those small towns one may see in a movie theater, except there were thousands of us.

I especially like to dedicate this to my loving parents, Marge and Mickey, for teaching me to work hard and appreciate what I have in life. It's a lesson I will never forget.

I don't know where I would be without my friends on Facebook who encouraged me to push on. Their feedback was a tremendous help to me. One of those Facebook friends was someone I had never met. His name was James Millaway. Not only was he encouraging, but he provided excellent feedback when he read my posts. We had so much in common; it was scary. Sadly, he passed away two Christmases ago. I had wanted so badly to get a finished book into his hands.

INTRODUCTION

Did you ever wonder where the years went? Sometimes I feel as if I am still 21. However, today, I'm 68 years old. I know for sure that I had one hell of a life. It all started back in 1960 as I attended a Catholic grade school. It was there that I learned the fear of God as a chalked-up eraser sped by my forehead. Yes, the joys of life were plenty.

These are true stories compiled over the last sixty-four years, and real names are used throughout.

We lived in a row house community with many families who had kids our age. We had parks to play in, but we also invented many street games. How many people do you know who could catch a football between two parked automobiles? Do you think those suburban kids had it all? Hardly!

This book is a series of essays that brought me back to those earliest times, a special place where I learned to play with many others while respecting my elders. We had a community with many corner stores, two big movie theaters, and a drive-in movie. We could do any kind of shopping within the neighborhood, including groceries, toys, records, clothing, shoes, paint. You could even buy Easter chicks at the local Murphy's department store!

I hope you enjoy the ride as I take you from the streets of Southwest Philly to the Jersey Shore, where many of our neighbors took their vacations.

ACKNOWLEDGMENTS

I owe a debt of gratitude to my editor, Judy Baehr. Not only did she keep me going in the right direction, but she also encouraged me to expand the material where it was most needed. She was truly wonderful to work with.

I also need to thank many of my friends who inspired me to move forward and keep writing. Jim Capobianco and Jim Brennan provided me with some early editing before I pursued writing a book. One of my closest friends, Andrew Buchanan, helped with editing and provided me with a title. He also proofread my manuscript.

In particular, I'd like to mention one of my classmates, Marian Mooney Fahy, who convinced me to write down these tales while I still had my memory. It was great advice, given that both she and I took care of relatives with dementia. I saw my dad struggle mightily with this disease.

My cousin Kathy Bakanauskas provided many pictures I've included in this book. Many thanks for her kindness!

Kudos to neighbors Sophia Smith Duffy and Michael Parente, who provided me with information regarding the story "Mario the Barber." Sophia was one of the girls who had her bangs trimmed by Mario. Mike put me in touch with Mario's son Jim, otherwise known as JimmyJoe.

Many thanks to Donna Cupps Moshinski for providing gaps about her brother's life before moving to our Southwest Philly area. Donna also provided me with pictures of her brother as he aged.

Thank you to Kathleen Peca Mancaruso, who provided pictures of her family and filled in some historical gaps concerning her family.

Thank you to Phyllis Mundy-Wagner for giving my manuscript a read and the beautiful letter she wrote to me about the book.

Thanks to the many friends I have written about. I appreciate that they have a good sense of humor and were happy to participate in this effort.

Finally, I owe my wife, Donna, a debt of gratitude as she not only helped me in many ways but watched me spend hours in our study as I composed the material. She also read and critiqued my manuscript. I couldn't have done this without her.

TABLE OF CONTENTS

1

Growing Up In Our Neighborhood

Mom and me

I grew up in Southwest Philadelphia.

Southwest Philadelphia is the southern portion of the city lying west of the Schuylkill River. It is bounded on the north by Baltimore Avenue, Fiftieth, and Forty-Ninth Streets; on the west by Cobbs and Darby Creeks, which separate Philadelphia and Delaware Counties; on the south by the Philadelphia International Airport; and on the east by the Schuylkill River. It takes in the neighborhoods of

Kingsessing, Elmwood, Paschall, and Eastwick Avenues. My home was between Buist Avenue and Lindbergh Boulevard within the Elmwood zone, near 62nd Street.

It's funny, but a pleasant neighborhood doesn't happen automatically. It takes a mix of working parents, community churches, small stores that cater to their customers, and neighbors caring about each other. People who live in stable neighborhoods care about their properties. Whether they are renting or buying, they mow their lawns, clean their sidewalks, steps, porches, and windows, and keep the drapes or blinds spiffy. It is all hard work and sacrifice.

There were fifty-two houses on our block. I knew almost every one of our neighbors. While there were many young families with children, plenty of older folks lived there, too. They were the security cameras of our day, keeping both toddlers and teens in line. Eyes and ears seemed to be everywhere. We recognized that they watched over us and that if we did something wrong, our parents would find out about it. Although we didn't grow up in a bubble, we still felt protected.

Daytime brought out the best of our ingenuity. Kids built their own scooters comprising a wooden beer case, a two-inch high by three-inch wide by a three-feet long piece of wood, and a pair of skates, the kind we used to attach to our sneakers. We nailed the crate to the stud's front end; then attached a set of wheels to the stud's underside, both front and back. Handles made from mom's old broomstick were hooked up to the box. We added soda caps to the front of the container to display style and individuality.

On the hottest days, someone's dad would open the fireplug, allowing children on the street to get a good soaking and ease the temperature's intensity. I remember hearing Ed Hurst and the Steel Pier Show playing through open windows on Saturdays. It was the first time I listened to The Rolling Stone's song, "Satisfaction."

Summer nights in our neighborhood brought on a fresh assault of heat and humidity. Stale air permeated the area unless you were one of the lucky ones with air conditioning. Most people in those days had window fans that just blew the hot air around the house. Many neighbors sat outside on their steps, patios, or porches and talked the night away, mainly to catch whatever outdoor breeze was available. During the 1960s, it wasn't uncommon for folks to knock on your door and be invited inside to chat. We were all like family then. We anxiously awaited Jolly Roger's Ice Cream or the pizza truck to arrive with nighttime goodies. Thankfully, my mom loved both.

Kids would chase lightning bugs throughout the evening, capturing them and putting them into glass jars with punctured lids. This created temporary lighting flashlights to guide their way. The little flying buggers didn't fare very well, even though the holes in the top allowed them to breathe. On some nights, the fireplug wrench often came out again to give us an old-fashioned cool-down before bedtime.

Ours was a neighborhood where most houses had backyards that faced each other, with alleys between. After midnight, garbagemen would come up the path and collect refuse to sell to pig farms in New Jersey, unleashing a god-awful stench into the early morning atmosphere if they left the lid off the cans, which was often. But walk two blocks away, and you'd discover the aroma of gravy and meatballs cooking into the night, the savory vapors kissing the air as they escaped through open windows. You knew that you entered the neighborhood called "Little Italy." Though most pleasing to me was the smell of fresh-baked rolls coming from Mattera's bakery, just across the street from Our Lady of Loreto Church.

We lived during a time when doctors made house calls. The doctor typically brought his modest black bag containing a stethoscope, thermometer, cold medication, and sharp-pointed syringes to dispense penicillin, the cure for most childhood diseases. I never received a shot at home, but it was nice to have a professional verify that I was legitimately sick and write me a note for school. Those stern blue-robed ladies at Saint Barnabas Elementary School would accept nothing less. Milk deliveries came straight to our door two days a week, and we also got the Philadelphia Evening Bulletin daily.

My sister's friends used to mimic the Doo-Wop groups of the 1950s. Jake, Frog, Den, and Ray would sing on the corner at night, or at least until the cops came. I recall arguing with Jake about the importance of the lead singer versus the background singers. I insisted that the Four Tops would be nothing without their lead vocalist, Levi Stubbs. Jake shot me a glare that suggested I should be executed for such a stance.

I credit my sister for giving me my love of music. She was four years older than me and spun late 1950 tunes together with the splendid melodies of the 1960s. The songs of that time have stayed with me forever. I remember going to bed with a transistor radio next to my ear. It always comforted me. Even today, I listen to tunes while I write.

The boys played sports all day long, including stepball, stickball, boxball, and wireball, all of which required a pimple ball. We dabbled with chase games, such as Kick the Can, Release, and Hide and Seek.

I remember watching the girls playing Hopscotch, chalking pavement areas with squares in various colors to hop about. They also jumped rope, playing Double Dutch, timing their jumps to avoid two ropes twirled one after the other.

Come winter, there were snowball fights, sledding, football games played in the big park, jumping on the back of cars and buses for a quick ride, and shoveling pavements and steps for a little extra money. We had days off from school resulting in wearing old, heavy rubber boots held together by a series of metal clips. You could neither run nor walk very well in these awkward, poorly balanced boots. They did keep your feet dry, though, and that made mom happy.

We would terrorize the poor guys selling Christmas trees at the old Polish church near 63rd and Dicks Avenue during the Christmas season. Usually, we would sneak into the facility at night and crawl behind the trees leaning against the auditorium walls and pushing them over. Because we were small, the tree salesmen had a hard time catching us. Picture trying to track a dog running behind the trees. It wasn't bad enough the men had trouble keeping warm; now, they had to chase the young kids and restack the fallen trees.

For my Catholic classmates, we understood that whatever happened at St. Barney's grade school stayed there! Our teachers, nuns of the sisters, Servants of the Immaculate Heart of Mary (IHM) order, kept their students under control. I never told my mom how often they rapped my knuckles or what trouble I was in because I knew that, however awful it was at school, I'd get twice that at home. My parents both had to work, so they purposely enrolled me in a Catholic institution, knowing that I would be around many kids, receive a solid education, and face discipline if required. I was lucky. In eight years, I avoided suspension or being sent to the office of the Mother Superior.

I cannot speak for the girls. They are a much different species, as I would come to learn throughout my life. In fact, I'm still trying to figure them out. My sister Denise was lukewarm about sharing her St. Barney's experience concerning the Holy Sisters. However, a few of my female classmates did tell me what they thought of the nuns. Some were critical. But I think we all agreed that we received a solid education.

Many public schools dotted the neighborhood. Though I cannot speak to the level of teaching conducted at these institutions, my non-Catholic friends seemed to do well. Everyone used their facilities to play intramural sports, so there were always plenty of activities to keep us active and out of trouble.

Various parents served as our coaches, whether we played Midget football, Little League baseball, or basketball. I remember playing as a fifty-two-pound right guard for the Elmwood Athletic Club. A guy named Danny Harrell coached almost every kid who came from Southwest Philadelphia. He and other men contributed their time to ensure that we all learned to play and work as a team, not to mention teaching us the all-important courtesies of sportsmanship. I cannot thank enough the guys who taught me as a youngster: besides Danny, Johnny Walker, Jake Fleisher, Bill Carboni, Johnny Nace, Al Baldwin, and John Tiernan, just to name a few, helped us kids learn responsibility and accountability for each other, a lesson to which we cannot attach a price.

What made the neighborhood great? Many of the folks who lived in Southwest Philly could work close to home. Sizable companies like

General Electric, Westinghouse, Ryerson Steel, MAB Paints, Brill's Steel, and Breyer's Ice Cream were within walking distance or were a short trolley or bus ride from their homes. These firms paid well, providing security for its blue-collar workforce and enabling homeowners to live an enjoyable life, pay their mortgages, feed their families, support the neighboring businesses, and take a one-week vacation to the Jersey shore during the summer.

We could shop along Woodland Avenue, where you could buy anything you needed without ever having to use your car. Since shopping malls were non-existent during this time, the only high-end shopping existed in Center City, a trolley ride away. There you would find Wanamaker's, Strawbridge and Clothier, Gimbel's, and Lit Brothers.

We had the Benn and Benson movie theaters, which had double features on the weekends for entertainment. We also had the 61st Drive-In with their dollar-per-carload specials. Corner bars flourished, too: the Tumble Inn, Dee's, Eddie's Café, the Homestead, Cook's Pub, the Barrel Inn, Hastings, Bob's Grill, the Hut, the Greenway Tavern, and a few more I'm forgetting. We had a bowling alley, a roller skating rink, and quite a few places to eat, including the Robinson Diner, Theodoe's, the Avenue Restaurant, and the Big House, to name a few, and too many cheesesteaks and hoagies shops to mention. A local bakery, Mattera's, provided homemade rolls daily to the local residents and small sandwich establishments.

What a privilege it was to grow up in this small-town atmosphere. I sincerely believe that we were blessed. Our Southwest Philadelphia neighborhood upbringing was no accident. It was a concerted effort by all to raise our families the right way. We had it all; unity, caring, responsibility, and accountability. Those people, those places, those things that happened, helped mold us all. Even today, when we meet at events, it is recognizable just how lucky we were. You can see it in the eyes of our neighbors and friends; the smiles and laughter simply endure. I've always appreciated what I have in life. I am so thankful for the great families, great teachers, great friends, and great neighbors we had. I owe them all.

2

Welcome To Saint Barney's

Saint Barnabas Elementary School

In September 1960, I walked into St. Barnabas Catholic School for the first time. At the very impressionable age of six, I was one of a large group of 180 students or about sixty kids for each of the three classes entering first grade that year.

I remember my mother waking me on that early fall morning. Mom told me to put on a pair of trousers and a white shirt that she had ironed the night before. The finishing touch was a clip-on tie. With my shiny new shoes, I was ready to take on the world. Mom and I posed for a picture taken outside our house that morning. Little did I know I would lose her thirteen years later.

We never ate breakfast during the week, only on weekends. Mom had a full-time job, and I was never hungry in the morning. I noticed that mom had dressed for work, so I surmised that she was taking me to school, and I wouldn't be coming right back to our house. She and my dad had talked about school, and at first, the idea had interested me. As we approached the chain-link fence of the schoolyard, I heard a buzz of activity ahead. Groups of children were lined up on the blacktop; the boys were dressed like me; some even wore suits. The girls were dressed in their green and gold-colored St. Barney uniforms. My anticipation of the fun they'd promised mounted, and I thought, *Look at all those kids!* Mom gave me a kiss and said goodbye. Some parents heard their children start to cry when they left the area. Like little soldiers at Boot Camp, we marched down the walkway and into the building now separated by our first-grade classes.

Sister Marie Roberts introduced herself and asked us to raise our hands if we knew how to make the Sign of the Cross. My hand stayed put; I recognized this practice only as "In the Name of the Father." But I wasn't the only one with a nomenclature problem.

Another student did not respond to his own name being called out during roll call, a routine that would become a part of every day. Apparently, no one in John's family ever addressed him by his baptismal name. As Sister continued to ask for John Mossman, she heard only crickets. The child in question sat there, wide-eyed and frightened, while others pointed at him. The tension mounted. He finally stood, looking around, bewildered, and announced, "My name is Jackie."

Parental dreams of higher education crashed and burned; however, later in life, John scored so high on an intelligence test that he received military training to track the enemy while serving our country in Thailand during the Vietnam War.

By the end of that first week, I realized that my parents had scammed me when they'd said it would be fun. The lives of my classmates and I would be changed for the next eight years. This wasn't fun. In my mind, in the minds of my friends, decades before *Ferris Bueller's Day Off* would enter our consciousness, we found ourselves trapped in this daily hell with these stern, dark-robed women who wore heavy, odd-looking religious construction boots. And what was that thing on their heads? Did they even have foreheads?

In the first couple of weeks in school, I shared a hybrid-desk unit with a boy named Joseph. This unique design combined two seats built into one piece of furniture, which bolted to the floor. Joined to my partner for the entire year, regardless of whether he carried head lice, or fleas, or had terrible manners, I came to know Joseph as The Classmate from Hell. An attention-craving, needy child, he had been dropped by Satan into our room to challenge us quiet kids just trying to behave. Joseph gave me a hard time all day long.

I recall one afternoon when I was doing my best to ingest the new material coming my way, not paying any mind to Joseph when he stuck me in the ass with a tack. My reaction was to reach over and shove him. I pushed him so hard that he flew out of his seat and hit the big, gray, cast-iron radiator below the windows across the aisle.

Now I've stepped in it? Only two weeks into the school year, and here I was, a shy and quiet kid fighting in class. What was worse, in early September in Southwest Philadelphia, the weather was still hot. All of us still wore short-sleeved shirts, including Joseph. I wasn't aware that he already had a big scrape on his left elbow. As he hit the radiator, the scab ripped off, opening his wound, and blood spewed like a geyser. There was so much blood that it looked as if I had shot him. After cradling that spawn of Satan in her arms, Sister charged me and unleashed fury, the likes of which I'd never seen at home. Sister resembled a short but feisty bowling ball with boxer's arms and penguin's feet. She worked me over for about ten minutes, never knowing that I hadn't started it.

I was to find out that Joseph had two older brothers at St. Barnabas. A year later, a nun I didn't know brought his next oldest brother into our second-grade class. The purpose seemed to be to teach him a lesson and, presumably, to scare the hell out of us at the same time. [I'm guessing that his teacher had had enough of him.] When he reached our teacher's desk, to our complete shock, she pulled him over her knee onto the desk, dropped his pants to expose his bare butt, and spanked him right in front of us. It wasn't long after that incident that the family got expelled from our school. We never saw our nemesis again.

In those days, it was assumed that the children would be educated per the Catholic doctrine; thus, we would study religion and your basic courses such as spelling, reading, writing, arithmetic, geography, science, and history. Our parents would also allow the nuns to discipline the kids. For example, if you got caught talking to a classmate during a teacher's session, you may end up writing on the blackboard 100 times, "I must not talk in class." Some nuns threw erasers at you;

others would hit you with a pointer or a yardstick. It all depended on the disturbance you caused. There were no laws written down about discipline. School life is much different today since many schools do not allow corporal punishment.

I was too young to understand that, considering the number of kids in these classes, it was inevitable that there would be some problems along the way. As with everything else in life, though, you learn to adjust. We came to see these chaotic moments as a break in the inaction. The inexorable daily grind of memorizing multiplication tables and Catechism passages for long periods can try a kid's patience. We needed at least two to three minor disturbances during the day to keep the juices flowing. It was a lesson I would take with me throughout the eight years I attended this school.

Welcome to St. Barney's!

3

My Hyperactive Buddy

Joey Peca

This story began in 1958. Playing outside my house would introduce me to a lifelong set of friends, many of whom would become my classmates in two years. We spent our days exploring the streets, alleys, and fields of our vibrant neighborhood. One of these buddies, albeit an older one, would live a tough yet short life. His name was Joseph, but we called him Joey.

Joey Peca grew up across the street from me. Imposing even at a young age, Joey had close-cropped black hair that contrasted with his pale white skin. A full-blooded Italian, he always called me Michael, much like my aunts and cousins on my mother's side. As a rule, if someone screamed "Michael!" in a loud voice in my vicinity, I was either misbehaving, in imminent danger, exercising my selective hearing, or otherwise causing problems. During the 1960s, too, the nuns always called you by your proper Christian name, even as they came after you. If you had your face slapped, knuckles cracked, or your hair pulled, at least you knew that they'd paid respect to your name.

One day in the spring of 2019, my sister and I had lunch with our former next-door neighbor, Mary Frances, better known as "Boopsie." As we spoke over our meal, she told me the following story: Her mom, Franny, met a distant relative from her side of the family, who also happened to be a Catholic nun. She and Boopsie were picking her up around the corner on 62nd Street and Lindbergh Boulevard. The two greeted the Holy Sister early in the afternoon as she exited the *G* bus. A quick five-minute walk would take them to Franny's home. However, on the way, they would have to pass the Peca household at the end of the block. Young Joey and Boopsie both were five years old. While she exuded a quiet, respectful manner, he was precocious, an active, in-your-face child who clamored for attention.

As the group approached Robinson Street, something seemed amiss at the Peca home. The Peca's had a beautiful bay window at the front of the house. The sizeable middle portion was stationary, while two operable side windows opened out to allow extra air. As they walked along the boulevard, Franny looked up, gasped, and came to an abrupt halt.

Joey had climbed onto the window ledge from inside his living room and was swinging out on one of the moveable side windows. An adventurous little bedbug, Joey was bare-ass naked as he swung out over the patio. Franny was horrified. Worse, she was embarrassed because her presumably holier relative saw this irrepressible young boy performing his best Johnny Weissmuller imitation, Tarzan *sans* loincloth. Just then, and perhaps by divine Providence, Joey lost his grip, falling out onto his grassy lawn in full view of the neighbors. Shocked and humiliated, he ran to the door.

As Boopsie told me this story, I really could visualize Joey doing this. It was right up in his wheelhouse. I figured that the nude aspect must be some kind of Italian thing. (I say this because my current neighbor, whose also Italian, had a nickname for his oldest son – "Naked Frankie." I never questioned the reason for this; I just figured that they had an operable bay window, too.)

Boopsie explained that Joey did this often, a revelation that did not surprise me. I knew Joey too well.

In later years, Joey and I played baseball on the big field up the street. The large, open park separated row homes on Dewey and Robinson streets, creating a spacious recreation area for the kids. The total length of the grounds measured five rowhouses, or approximately one hundred feet – our own miniature version of *Field of Dreams*. Four end properties marked the perimeter of the playground, two on each street. I imagine that the designers of this neighborhood had assumed that a certain number of children would live here and calculated these large spaces to accommodate their outdoor activities.

On one corner, representing home plate, was the Ellis residence. In left field stood the house where the Pintos lived. They were elderly sisters. The Ellis daughter was in my class at St. Barney's. Both of these property fronts faced Robinson Street.

In center field sat the first household that faced Dewey Street. Sometimes the neighbors would get excited if the older kids participated in the ballgame. And they had a point: they were afraid that their windows would get broken. However, given the skill level of most of us younger kids, this area was the least likely spot to hit the ball for distance. The last property marked the right field boundary. The front of this place pointed to Dewey Street, and any ball hit close to this structure would be a foul ball. This layout gave the playground its perfect square shape.

Besides the attractive landscape, concrete sidewalks ran the width of the grounds, located alongside the border dwellings. Another paved walkway split the park into two equally sized grassy fields.

One afternoon, we chose sides, laid out the bases, and began the game. Early in the fourth inning, Joey came to the plate. As he was a dead pull hitter to left field, the only house in jeopardy was the Pinto's. Joey never realized his own strength. Not the most agile of athletes, he had a strong arm and hit for power. I was defending second base when Joey unleashed a solid line drive that soared over the outfielder's head and crashed through the double-paned glass that provided light and ventilation for the elderly sisters' dining room. Although we were older now, we were still young kids. None of us had any money, so we all scattered like cartoon roaches darting under the refrigerator when someone turned on the kitchen light. Perhaps a dad or two paid to repair the broken window, but I never knew for sure whether the Pintos ever received any compensation for the damage we did to their home. I can only hope that they did. I felt sorry for them.

All these years later, despite the naggings of my Catholic guilty conscience, Boopsie, my sister Denise, and I enjoyed a hearty laugh looking back at these memories of our childhood in that beautiful neighborhood. All of our parents have died and have sacred duties now. The main character of this story, Joey, left us five years ago. This allowed Joey time to quickly slip fifty bucks to St. Peter so he could enter the Pearly Gates. Now that's a jury I'd love to sit on. Carmen and Eva Peca will need to defend why their youngest boy distracted the angels with lavish bowls filled with popcorn and Godiva chocolates.

Rest in Peace, my friend!

4

Mommy, Why Is The Sky Different Colors?

Mom and me (1956)

The year was 1962. At this time, we were still heating our home with coal. In fact, many properties in Southwest Philly were equipped with bins used to store this precious fuel. I'll never forget the days when the coalman arrived at the house with his huge dump truck to make a delivery. The sound produced by a ton of dark gray, brown, or shiny black rocks sliding down a metal chute resembled that of an avalanche roaring through your front basement window and falling into the storage bin.

To add fuel to the furnace, you had to get a load of coal from the bin and walk it to the heater, which, in our case, was about fifteen feet away. A cast iron door protected the actual burner within the large heating unit and covered the firebox where we placed the coal. Our parents taught us as children how to load the burner. To protect yourself, you needed a heavy glove to handle the door. To visualize this process, I would direct you to the movie *Titanic*, either the black-and-white original or the sappy love-story version with Leonardo DiCaprio and Kate Winslet. Both films have a scene showing boilermakers shoveling coal into the ship's firebox, built into a much larger boiler.

My mom and our neighbor, Eva Peca, worked for the Chilton Publishing Company when my friend Joey and I were in grade school. Once the class let out, we could play for two hours before either of our moms arrived home. This gave us plenty of time to experiment with the basement furnace. Joey's idea was to toss toys into the burner. We brainstormed. I concurred, picking plastic bowling pins fashioned after characters based on The Flintstones, an early 1960s cartoon show.

Fred Flintstone and his next-door neighbor, Barney Rubble, live during the Stone Age and work in a quarry. Fred, who wears orange caveman clothing, is of medium height, with black hair and a stocky build. Barney, who wears a brown outfit, is short and stout with blond locks. Both manage to work barefoot and sleeveless even though there are perilous rocks all around them. Each has a beautiful spouse. Fred's wife, Wilma, is a redhead who always dresses in white. Barney's wife, Betty, is a vision in blue with black hair. Imagine the color scheme when they add a pet dinosaur to the mix. Dino is Fred and Wilma's prehistoric pet. He is strikingly colored purple. Oh, what a range of colors to toss into a furnace!

What motivates kids to throw plastic toys into a raging fire? A psychiatrist would best answer that question, but for now, I offer this explanation. Joey was a boy who challenged the rules. He was that kid who, told to stay out of the deep end of the pool, would continue to creep further into the deeper water, one step at a time. Me? I was the gullible dope, curious to see what would happen. So, without another thought, Joey and I threw the toys into the burner.

At age 64, having worked as a welder for eighteen years, I know what happens when materials burn. Steel, for example, absorbs heat, turns orange, and melts. Plastic, however, is more complicated. It doesn't break down similarly to other substances, making disposal of it rather difficult. Fire departments deal with many housing materials and the hazards they can cause. Burning these substances emits chemical elements into the atmosphere. Over time, scientists have blamed attempts to get rid of plastic for harming the environment. Needless to say, our treatment of the environment in 1962 was nowhere near as big an issue as it is today.

We two young, precocious "researchers" never blinked. Hell, we grew up surrounded by questionable environmental endeavors, Atlantic and Gulf oil refineries among them. General Electric had a three-block facility in the most populated part of our neighborhood. Almost half of the local dads had jobs there. Because of this electrical plant, God only knows how many poisonous PCBs (polychlorinated biphenyls) floated through our atmosphere daily. Not to mention that we kids chased the mosquito trucks that drove through the area just for fun, breathing in the toxic fumes. We drank from garden hoses and bought pretzels from street vendors. We had no fear.

As the celluloid bowling pins hit the flames, colorful smoke spewed a rainbow of pigments to the top of our chimney. On average, sky hues comprised whites, reds, light blues, and orange. But deep purples, navy blues, and hideous greens did not fit the usual color palette. God only knew what chemicals escaped to the open air with them.

My parents never questioned me about the missing toys. No neighbors complained about the kaleidoscope of colors or the nuclear cloud cover hovering over their houses for hours. No agencies arrived with men dressed in hazmat suits to investigate the cause of the pollution. Life continued in our not-so-typical Southwest Philly neighborhood, where Joey was already planning what we would be doing next.

5

Mario The Barber

Mario Braccille

When I was a kid, a barber named Mario had a shop that sat at the corner of 61st Street and Lindbergh Boulevard in the heart of Southwest Philadelphia. It was a tiny place, with perhaps three working chairs, and Mario worked alone. All of the neighborhood kids went to Mario's, even though we had to cross a busy intersection to get there. Many trucks and buses passed along this route, making it hazardous to pedestrians. Endless row houses, on-street parking, and motorized behemoths combined to create poor visibility for little ones. I had to walk a block from my house to get to Mario's.

Mario seemed tall, but then everybody's tall when you're a kid. He always wore an immaculately white, short-sleeved barber's shirt with long black slacks and matching black shoes. He had a pleasant demeanor, was easy to talk to, but had not a strand of hair to call his own. The top of his head looked like a shiny skin-toned bowling ball. As a kid, I found it strange that a bald guy would cut hair for a living. It made as much sense to me as a blind referee calling a live football game.

For as many child customers as he had, Mario's clientele included adults as well. And that's where the story gets interesting. Older men would arrive with newspapers in hand, remove their hats, take a seat, and strike up conversations with the barber. Some of these tales were quite startling to the young ears that would absorb them. I remember overhearing a low, raspy voice saying, "They got Johnny last night."

Mario took it in, never changing the expression on his face or extending the conversation any further as if he had morphed into a Catholic priest, sworn to keep his parishioners' sins to himself. For us kids, it was thrilling, our own inside ticket to the clandestine world of the local Mob. And much like the Mafia "wise guys" who had to observe the unwritten law of *omerta*, we kept those conversations to ourselves, never spilling the beans to our folks or, God forbid, a nun or a priest.

We would listen to the men plan their weekly poker games, talk of going to the horse races, discuss the daily bookie's number, or mention "hot" items for sale in the local bars. Our parents never discussed these topics at home. It was us kids who were part of the action, privy to the most private of revelations. I found it fascinating. In all probability, had you patronized most of the South Philly barbershops that existed during the 1960s, you would have heard similar stories. (And don't mistake that raspy voice used by Marlon Brando when he filmed *The Godfather* as his own invention. He was a "method" actor, so he was sure to have done his research. I wouldn't have been surprised to hear him thank his barber and admit in some award acceptance speech that he had perfected this voice while getting his childhood haircuts. (Unfortunately, Marlon shunned those award shows, particularly in 1972, when he won Best Actor for *The Godfather* and sent American Indian Sacheen Littlefeather in his place to address the American Indian Rights Movement.)

I remember, too, as a little boy, seeing well-dressed men hanging around the Italian Club near where I lived. When the kids approached, we could hear the men switch from speaking English to Italian. For example, a typical conversation would sound like this, "Hey Frankie, how you feeling? Ah, you know Chico, Mezza Mezza." (Translation: I take the good with the bad.) The older guys smoked cigars that reeked from a block away, ruining the sweet smell of a tomato pie baking in the local pizzeria. It could spoil a summer evening. There was an Italian Club on the next corner from my grandmother's house in South Philly. Guys in sharply pressed silk suits would linger in front of the building at all hours of the day and night throughout the week, leading one to believe that, unlike our fathers, these dudes didn't go to work. They would roll dice and play cards. Or they would just break each other's balls – over cars, clothing choices, or girlfriends. I wondered how they could afford all those expensive suits without having jobs.

A few years ago, I learned that Mario used to take the young girls into his shop to trim their bangs as requested by their mothers. To say that our neighborhood was affluent would be a lie. Mario understood how it was and tried to help as many people as he could. He also served as an usher at St. Barnabas Church. With his commitment to our community, it is no wonder that his business flourished for so many years.

I don't recall exactly when my visits with Mario ended. I don't remember if or when he retired. He could be sitting in some small town in Iowa, a member of the Witness Protection Program for all I know.

My haircuts were far more compelling back then when all I had to do was sit still and look uninterested. Despite whatever was or wasn't going on in Mario's life, I always found him to be a kind and honorable man who gave me a terrific haircut. And during these times, being "honorable" carried a lot of weight.

6

Games We Played In The Winter

Joey Peca, snowball master

Joey Peca's house sat on the corner of our block, less than fifty feet from my home. He was older than I by one year and was ahead of me in school, too. Tall, dark, and broad-shouldered, he would have made a great outside linebacker had he chosen to play football. He wasn't a natural athlete; nevertheless, he still had some special skills. For example, he could throw a baseball for both accuracy and distance. He used this particular skill to master the art of throwing a snowball. And that is where this story begins.

Unlike the rest of us snowball jockeys, Joey didn't just aim at a moving car or truck. He thought that was far too easy. No, Joey took a more scientific approach to his strategy to harass and torment unsuspecting drivers. He would estimate a car's distance away, calculate the wind speed, and throw the snowball straight above the road on which the vehicle was traveling. His goal was, with impeccable timing, to land the object right on the roof of the oncoming automobile. The noise it made would jangle one's nerves, potentially causing an accident.

I considered Joey an innovator, ahead of his time, and far more knowledgeable in geometry and physics than anybody ever acknowledged. However, the Catholic nuns at St. Barnabas Grade School might disagree with this description, considering the amount of torture he inflicted on them daily.

One day, it snowed late into the evening. Given the eight inches of white stuff we awoke to the following morning, we had the day off from school, and my younger cousin, Vince, came to my house. We rounded up the usual suspects and gathered on the front steps of Joey's house to make plans for our afternoon activities. We debated whether to go sledding, play tackle football in the park, or throw snowballs at cars.

As we deliberated, Joey lovingly built the perfect snowball. Much like a great pizza chef, kneading his dough to the right consistency, Joey packed his mound of snow to the proper density. He sculpted the snowball with the kind of precision associated with building the finest meatball, having the correct ratio of beef, pork, and veal along with just the right touch of bread, garlic, parsley, Pecorino Romano cheese, and cream. Joey left the guys on the steps, still talking while walking to the edge of his grass. Before any of us realized what was happening, he unleashed a mighty throw into the sky.

I knew what to expect; poor Vince had no clue. Snowball and car roof connected with a thundering crash, and we all went running for cover. My house was close by, and I was faster than my cousin. The car driver that Joey had hit made a U-turn on Lindbergh Boulevard and headed towards 2600 Robinson Street. But while he was executing the corner turn, the vehicle slid, trapping Vince part-way up the block. I had made it home and positioned myself on my knees in front of the living room window, from where I could peek through the blinds. The scene unfolding was a keeper, like high-definition television before its time.

As the auto sped up the street, Vince realized that he couldn't outrun it. He stopped and reversed direction, forcing the vehicle to do the same. I could see in the high-definition image that the automobile had a stick shift, chains on its tires, and a driver operating his car on a snow-slicked blacktop. My cousin, bless his heart, was running for his life wearing those awful 1960s-vintage snow boots. We had difficulty walking in those things, let alone trying to run.

As Vince careened down the street, that driver tracked him like a heat-seeking missile, matching him move for move. I imagined the frustration he must have felt, engaging the clutch, shifting gears, and sliding in the snow, trying to stay with his elusive prey. I giggled so hard that my mother came out of the kitchen to find out why. This was more entertaining than a Three Stooges episode!

I was in tears but couldn't let my mom see why I was laughing. If I had told her, poor Vince would only have gotten deeper into trouble. He was already dodging a car; did my cousin really need his aunt coming down on him, too? Peeved at me for not giving up my secret, she slapped me on the head with a *Life* magazine. I laughed even harder, which only made matters worse. Mom just got angrier, and she had no idea that we'd planned to throw snowballs at cars that day. Geez, my dad drove a cab for a living. God only knows how he would have reacted if she'd told him about our antics.

She never found out why. To this day, it was worth it. I did enough bad things already. Why would I stack the deck against me even more? She already called me a miserable kid; why add that I threw snowballs at cars, potentially causing an accident on the boulevard? Frankly, not giving her more reason to land on me allowed me to grow out of this dangerous winter pastime without consequences. I was lucky.

As fate would have it, the guy in the car happened to live on Vince's street, a few blocks away. So, he recognized Vince anyway, although Vince didn't recognize him. My cousin got caught and had to stay in the house for the next two weekends with no allowance when all he'd intended to do was pay me a visit and have fun in the snow. For my part, I had secured a winter memory for a lifetime, and when it plays in my head with every winter snowfall, it brings a smile to my face.

As for Joey, while this mad ruckus went on outside, our snowball sculptor sat in the warmth and comfort of his mom's kitchen, munching on a bologna sandwich!

7

Christmas Mass At St. Barnabas Church

Saint Barnabas

The year was 1964, the day, December 25th. On this frigid Winter morning, I would attend my first Christmas Mass as an altar boy. This Mass was significant. For days before, we held practices, made confessions, and spiffed up our cassocks and surplices, the latter with wide pleats that mom had to iron. We covered almost every conceivable detail with the proverbial fine-toothed comb, ensuring no lapses would occur in our preparation for this special celebration.

The Mass began at 5:30 on Christmas morning, necessitating my mother waking me up an hour earlier. I remember thinking, here I was, ten years old, waking up in the middle of a pitch-black night, when other children have nestled all snug in their beds, dreaming of presents beneath the tree. And I had to go to work!

The altar boys had to be there extra early. No one wanted to face the wrath of the Catholic nuns for missing this special event. In Catholic liturgy, this celebration was a High Mass, which meant that several priests and deacons would help with the observance. The celebrants were reverent in their white chasubles with gold embroidery. As we made our way to church that morning, I couldn't suppress my yawns, a clear sign that I hadn't had enough sleep. I wasn't alone, however; droopy, heavy eyelids defined most of the faces of us boys that morning. As altar servers, we sat in the church's front pews, which seemed enormous back then. The solemnity, the beautiful red poinsettias and festive evergreen branches, the flickering candles shining so bright, as if the whole congregation had put coins into the collection box, and the statues, basking in reflective lighting, looking alive and ready to join in the celebration at any moment. The swelling organ music engulfed the entire church, and the angelic choir anthems made it seem like all of heaven had dropped in for a visit.

Christmas Eve, of course, is a time of celebration, too, whether you're ten years old or over eighty. You might be forgiven for overindulging while you're putting lights and tinsel on the tree, draping things just right. Most of us kids gorged on candy, pretzels, potato chips, and peanuts. We loaded up on sugary soda, too. That would have consequences.

On Christmas morning, after five hours of sleep, we found ourselves crammed together like tinned sardines for the better part of ninety minutes. Catholics go to Mass on Sundays but flock to church on special days such as Easter and Christmas, filling the pews, lining the side aisles, and standing in the back. As kids, we lived close by and could walk to church. However, anyone who had to drive to these holiday Masses found few to no parking spaces available, sending them scurrying onto neighboring streets that were already crowded. Cars would eventually double-park on Buist Avenue in front of the church, closing access to one of the lanes. Kindly District Twelve police officers would often look the other way rather than write a ticket on Christmas.

In the 1960s, the priest dispensed Holy Communion a single host at a time as he crossed the entire width of the sanctuary at the altar rail where people had lined up. Unlike today, when deacons and laypersons help distribute Communion, only the reverend was permitted to handle the tiny wafers which, by the mystery of Transubstantiation, had become the Body of Christ. Also, because we couldn't touch the Body of Christ even if it fell to the floor, everyone received the Communion host on the tongue.

The priest's sole assistant was an altar boy who followed him across the waiting line, placing a catch plate or paten under each person's chin. Altar servers had to know how to use that device because a Communion wafer would occasionally get away from the reverend. People's tongues are different lengths; some folks bite down too fast, startling the priest; or he just might be clumsy. As with priests, God did not create altar boys equal, either. They come in all shapes, sizes, and skillsets. Some were like a baseball starting nine, hands and eyes coordinated with the ability to complete a double play or snatch a host out of mid-air; others, awkward or absent-minded, belonged on the bench with the second-string players.

Almost everyone at the Mass received the host that night. For that reason, and for all the reasons stated, handing out Communion took a long time. We knelt in silence for what seemed an eternity. One altar boy, desperately in need of fresh air, threw up. And the stream landed right on the seat of the kid who sat in front of him. If things had not been bad enough already, the atmosphere had just become a lot less pleasant.

As the communicants were quietly reflecting and giving thanks to God, the celebrants were wrapping things up. At Saint Barnabas Church, there was a two-foot-wide aisle between the back of the tabernacle and the building's rear wall, not visible to the congregation. It was an isolated area where priests used to store extra-religious hardware. Suddenly, we heard a loud crash from behind the altar. We couldn't tell what had fallen. By sound, it had to be a chalice or a paten hitting a marble surface, but it was startling, as when a waiter or waitress drops a tray of food at a diner.

Occurring during one of the quietest times of the Mass, it caused a few of us kids to laugh. Stacked together like *Ritz* crackers as we were, with the odor of fresh vomit not far away, we knew that no nun would venture our way to punish the culprits. Also, we knew that a whole week of Christmas vacation would pass before we returned to school to face the wrath of the stern, dark-robed sisters.

As the ninety-minute celebration came to an end, the magic and mystery encapsulated into last prayers and well-wishes for everyone. We had arrived at this holiday event deep in the night but emerged with our souls refreshed, blessed, and released to the rising sun outside. Now we saintly altar boys could become real kids again, eager to see what lay under our Christmas trees! The choir sang "Joy to the World" as we marched down the long aisle of the church.

8

Santa Or The Neighbors

My sister Denise and I

In 1961, I was close to that age when children began to question Santa Claus's existence. This Christmas, at age 7, I would resolve the mystery by accident.

It's one thing when the kids in school talk about it; another when their older brothers and sisters spill the truth about the bearded, red-suited gift delivery man. The older kids are always a step ahead of their little brothers and sisters. While some are super careful not to give any secrets away, others are sloppy, forgetting the ears and sensitivity of their younger kin. A simple line like, "Mom and Dad shop for the presents," is a deal killer.

The previous year, my parents had sent me to bed early on Christmas Eve. Sometime after midnight, I heard a barrage of toy gunfire followed by my dad's bellowing laughter piercing through the quiet evening. My mother screamed, "Jesus Christ, Mickey, you're going to wake Michael!" My dad was putting together one of my gifts, a battery-operated toy machine gun. Apparently, it had jammed open, the noise waking up half the neighborhood. At that point, I suspected that something was amiss. However, the better part of me wanted to believe that Santa was for real. I wasn't ready to let go of this extraordinary feeling.

On a quiet Saturday morning, I went into my parents' bedroom only to make an intriguing discovery. They'd never barred me from entering their room; in fact, I had been in their sleeping quarters many times. My mother often sent me there to wake my father when he took an afternoon nap on the days when he was assigned to the second shift at work. When I remember back to that time in my life, now more than half a century later, I have to wonder what in God's name my parents were thinking.

As an adventurous sort and somewhat difficult to parent, I was about to show my folks just how much havoc a boy can create. I wasn't a hyperactive kid, but my older sister, Denise, behaved well by comparison. It was a dramatic contrast, one not in my favor. For example, Sister Mary Roberts had pummeled me to within an inch of my life in school. To get a nun's blood pressure up that high in a classroom, you needed to exhibit near maniacal behavior. Whether or not the poor woman might have had her own issues was beside the point. Lest you think I'm exaggerating, I had never sustained a beating, anything like that at home.

Perhaps my mother and father had told me not to go into their bedroom before Christmas, and I had ignored them? Sometimes it seemed that they just didn't understand child psychology. If they told us not to do something, we would get them every time. Let's face it: if parents learned to use that strategy effectively, their children would eat vegetables. Vegetable-eating problems solved! Just tell the little buggers that green beans taste nasty, and those kids will scarf them up like Hershey's Kisses.

As I entered my parents' room, I saw a blanket covering some very tall objects. In fact, they stood almost as high as the eight-foot ceiling. Looking under the heavy material, I discovered that the items were all the same toy, a seven-foot-long plastic bowling alley complete with pins and a ball. But why were there three of the same gifts? There were only two of us kids, Denise and me. And if they were meant for us, why had they not been wrapped?

I found out later that my mother and father and a set of neighbors had conspired to hide the presents. I imagined that mom and dad had lost a coin toss to decide who would take the responsibility to protect the stash. Or, maybe my parents, along with their co-conspirators, had taken an analytical approach to see who would cover up the gifts. I considered the data: the Reilly's had at least three kids. The Peca family also included three children. My parents had only Denise and me.

Using statistical analysis, any time there's an extra child in the house, there's a greater possibility of someone finding hidden goodies. My parents had won, or maybe I should say they'd *lost* the big contest, having taken on the responsibility of protecting the gifts for three neighboring families.

The Reilly kids' dad was a Philly policeman, so the dynamic in their household probably differed from ours. And, Mr. Reilly could have pulled rank on my father, on any given day, cop trumps cab driver. I would be remiss not to mention that the Peca family had other issues concerning storing the gifts at their property. Their youngest boy would have sniffed out any Christmas presents within hours of their placement under wraps. He caused enough trouble to make me look saintly. I can picture Joey setting up the bowling alley in his basement and playing with it until he got caught. His older, more mature brother, Carmen, would have sold the items had he found them.

It was, therefore, all but a foregone conclusion that my mother and father would store away the holiday toys.

This choice, although sound, was in error. I turned out to be the loose cannon. My sister was beyond the age of believing in Santa Claus. Besides that, I'd swear that that sweet goody-two-shoes rule-follower had the glow of a halo over her pale, freckled face and head. Not a single Catholic nun at our grade school would ever have come down on Denise; it never occurred in my eight years at St. Barnabas. Being a boy, my track record was much different. Although I didn't have a small red devil sitting on my shoulder, I still liked to talk, have fun, and couldn't control my laugh in class. After talking with my sister about our experience twenty years later, we discovered we had all different nuns at

Saint Barnabas. It made sense since we started school five years apart. Denise graduated from the school in 1963, while I finished in 1968.

Thus, my belief in Santa crashed and burned, but I only have myself to blame. That said, my love for the Christmas season remains intact. To this day, it is my favorite time of the year. However, I would advise parents to never engage in a coin toss with the neighbors regarding hiding presents and always wrap the gifts, so at least the suspense will still be there if, like me, your kids like to snoop around a bit.

9

A Classic Saturday At The Benn

The Benn Movie Theater
(Photo courtesy of Don Stott)

With so many children living in our neighborhood, I'm not shocked that our parents desired privacy during the weekend. (I always wondered why they wanted the young ones otherwise occupied, but that's a different story for another day.) Fifty cents per kid was cheap when it came to accomplishing that trick.

In the mid-1960s, the Benn Theater was one place where we spent our Saturdays. Between 63rd and 64th Streets on Woodland Avenue, the movie house had a surprising history. Rumor had it that

Hollywood actor W. C. Fields had lived in an apartment above the theater years ago.

The Benn offered double features each Saturday. The marquee usually listed at least one gladiator picture featuring actors whose lips moved out of sync with the voices. When we watched a movie like *Hercules Unchained* starring Steve Reeves, we never realized that he had spoken his lines in Italian. None of us kids knew what the word "dubbing" meant. It never once occurred to us that our favorite stars could deliver dialogue in other languages.

The second film might be a Jerry Lewis comedy or an Elvis Presley flick. Sometimes, Doris Day would star with Rock Hudson in a romantic farce. Often, the cinema might show one in a series of chilling horror pictures produced by Hammer Productions, with excellent British actors such as Vincent Price, Peter Cushing, or Boris Karloff. I'm sure some of the kids had nightmares after seeing those scary movies.

One lazy August morning, my friend Joey got the bright idea to "borrow" some chocolate candy from Jupiter's Department store and take it into the movies. This violated the rules. You can't bring food to the cinema with you. Most theaters had lobbies equipped with snack bars that served hot dogs, popcorn, soda, and sweets to generate added income. To my misgivings, Joey replied, "Michael, relax," and within minutes, he had hatched a plan to get me into the place since I had no money on me.

We walked behind the building to see which exit door I would stand. Once my friend had paid his ticket and gotten in, Joey would open the door from inside, allowing me to sneak in our bag of tasty treats to savor while we watched the flicks.

However, as I waited, I realized that we might have another problem. Once the film started, it would be pitch black in the playhouse but sunny outside. Also, the Benn was a two-sided movie house with a center aisle and aisles bordering the left and right sides. When Joey entered, he saw that one whole section of seating on the left side had been closed off. In the meantime, I was waiting outside, totally unaware that our clever plan could be about to fail.

After a few minutes, I heard Joey pushing on the exit door. With a quick rush of air, the door burst open, revealing me standing in glorious silhouette against the sky. The sunlight created a backdrop behind me, reminiscent of the scene in the horror movie *The Exorcist* when the priest arrived at the young girl's home possessed by the devil. As Father Merrin exited the taxi, a dazzling streetlamp emphasized his dark clothing, hat, and briefcase. It was brilliant cinematography, as the contrast between the darkness of the priest's wardrobe against the brightness of the lighting suggested a battle of good versus evil. Like the priest, albeit smaller and a confirmed sinner, I was a murky shadow against the blinding sun as I tried to sneak into the motion picture show with some fresh chocolates.

As I made my entrance, I could sense that the whole audience was watching every move I made, but as the actors' lips were already moving out of sequence with the soundtrack, I suspected they wouldn't miss any of the crucial plot points.

Meanwhile, Joey and I had dropped to all fours and begun crawling along the floor, mimicking soldiers navigating those obstacle courses found in basic training, trying to be discreet even though we had interrupted the entire movie-going experience. Scurrying about like water bugs, the ushers, aware that something was amiss, investigated the scene.

Calm against the chaos, my buddy and I crawled over half the width of the roped-off portion and sat in two of the seats. When the attendant came over and asked why we were sitting in the disallowed section, we played stupid. "We didn't know you couldn't sit over here," we claimed. He bought it. Maybe it was because we looked like the Dead End Kids, and the guy felt sorry for us. Or perhaps – more likely – he'd never seen me enter.

Anyway, the plan had succeeded, and, untroubled by pangs of conscience, Joey and I both enjoyed the movies for the price of a single ticket and one hijacked bag of candy on what was just another great Saturday afternoon in good old Southwest Philly.

10

Carmen, The Fireplug King

A typical Fire Hydrant

B ack in the 1960s, when music echoed through open windows on sunny afternoons, the fireplug was the next best thing to a swimming pool. Southwest Philly was a large area with at least one or two fireplugs on every block.

I'm sure that every block had a "fireplug king." Those who held this position came in all shapes and sizes and included dads, older brothers, uncles, distant cousins, even Jerry Blavat's "yon teens." The most important aspect of their job was securing and protecting the fireplug wrench, the tool custom made to fit the hydrant stem that activated the high-pressure release of the city water supply used to fight house fires. Owned by the police and fire department only, the wrenches weren't meant for public use. But we acquired them by two methods: one, some neighborhood men who worked as steelworkers could duplicate the tool using a casting mold; two, when cops chased the neighborhood kids, someone would steal the wrench from the unattended police car or fire truck.

The water from the fireplug was icy cold and seemingly endless. At eleven years old, we often rode our scooters into the mighty stream, which cleaned off all the mud and gunk that had built up throughout the week. Young teenage girls were frequently pulled in and dunked under the plug by their boyfriends or guys who liked them. We enjoyed days and nights of wet entertainment in that carefree time, never once considering what effect this might have had on the amount of water pressure in the immediate area. (That's what's so special about being a kid. Adults worry about that stuff.) For all we knew, that water would run forever – or at least until the cops showed up.

It was enough to keep the officers busy chasing down the open fireplugs while figuring out who possessed the fire department wrenches. We worked as a team, including the use of lookouts and wrench-hiding specialists who would quickly stash the tool, sometimes in a house or under a parked car, but often in the hedges. This group effort hampered Philly's Finest and their attempts to enforce the rules while providing sheer joy to the local youngsters through hours of wet, undisturbed fun.

Our "fireplug king" went by the name Carmen. Carmen lived across the street on the end property. You could ride down Lindbergh

Boulevard towards 62nd Street and make a right-hand turn onto 2600 Robinson in those days. The hydrant sat fifteen feet from the corner.

Carmen had some definite advantages. He was older, bigger, and stronger than we were. Still, most of all, he was blessed with a miraculous gift – an innocent grin – that would charm an unsuspecting motorist into driving fearlessly past the active fireplug. Carmen would smile at the intended victim, direct him through, then blast the side of his car with a tsunami-sized wave. His ability to manipulate streams of high-pressure water was uncanny. His timing and accuracy were spot-on, as drivers, some so dumb as to have left all their windows open, would get their vehicle soaked, sending us not-so-innocent bystanders into fits of laughter.

Reminiscent of actor Zachary Quinto's looks while sporting a thick head of jet-black hair, Carmen also had the buttock size and leg strength to master this fireplug feat. The trick was to force your butt over the fireplug outlet, then lower it enough to project a perfect stream of water over your back and into the night. Carmen, the master, could reach the front door across the street, splashing it as accurately as any car he would deluge with water. To see it was to appreciate it. That wave he generated flowed high above the asphalt, over the sidewalk, and up the steps before hitting the wooden entryway. The neighbors were not quite as impressed with Carmen's abilities as we were, to put it mildly. However, intimidated, much like the drivers whose cars were soaked, they offered little to no response, hoping the cops would round the corner at any minute and shut the plug off. I don't remember a single car driver ever challenging him.

Some years later, the city water utility's efficiency experts entered our lives, placing safe, water-reducing sprinkler heads on many fire hydrants. They assured that the children would still have a good time, but they took the rebellious aspect away. I felt sorry for the little tykes when I would drive through the streets. Yeah, they were getting wet. But no longer did the police chase kids or catch dads hiding the fire-plug wrench.

As an adult, I can't even imagine all the energy we used to use running from cops, leaping over fences, scooting up the small alleys while dogs screamed through the summer evenings. And when I hearken back to those days, I must smile as I remember Carmen, with that big grin on his face, waving the cars on, daring them to go forward.

11

Mom's Angel – Franny Kusner

Franny, her husband, Ed, and son, Joseph

The year was 1966. I was 12 and in sixth grade when my mother became ill. In her mid-thirties, she was in the prime of her life, still working full time at a job she loved, and the disease devastated her. It started when the fingers on her left-hand curled inward on their own and locked into place. It looked like a spasm or cramp that would strike suddenly then, after about five minutes of agony, settle down and subside, allowing her hand to return to normal. Mom had no control over these episodes. It would take three years for the doctors to diagnose her with multiple sclerosis (MS).

Beyond the spasms, her legs weakened, and her balance became compromised. She continued to work until one day she fell while rushing to cross Chestnut Street. Fortunately, a bus driver parked near the corner and aligned with the oncoming traffic, lay on his horn, hanging part-way out of his driver's side window to stop the cars. Mom was petrified, realizing she couldn't get up on her own. That day marked the end of her work career because she became too fearful of venturing outside independently. She still had no clue what ailed her.

Any illness of this nature affects the entire family. We all felt so bad for my mother, but little could be done to help her feel better physically. A vibrant and joyful woman who loved to sing and dance now could barely walk or hold up her own weight. None of us knew much about the disease. My sister Denise and I understood that we had to step up to help with household chores, food shopping, cooking, and doing the laundry. Dad handled it the best he could, but he was an old-school South Philly guy, the kind of man who holds his feelings inside. I can only imagine the heartache he felt when alone. We didn't know which way to turn or understand how disabled she might become, but none of us expected to lose her in seven short years.

At first, doctors thought that she suffered from both Bell's palsy and shingles. Before her diagnosis, she underwent several painful spinal taps, anything to find a clue to her symptoms. In the 1960s, magnetic resonance imaging (MRI) scanners were not available. Invented in the mid-1970s, after mom's death, MRI scans help to diagnose this disease today. If multiple sclerosis is active, meaning patients show symptoms, the machine can detect the nerves under attack. The nerve fibers, much like electrical cable, have an insulating layer or sheath called myelin, a white fatty substance that protects the nerve. It is this protective coating that MS compromises. Under an MRI scan, the myelin cover will sometimes reveal a moving coloration change that identifies the nerve under assault. The screening also detects lesions and scars left in the myelin insulation when the condition is inactive.

Although I learned to do many of the chores mom did to keep the house in order, there were special people all along the way who would help us manage. One of those folks was our next-door neighbor, Franny Kusner. The Kusners were terrific neighbors. Mom and Franny often spent time in the backyard while hanging clothes on the line. They laughed about the typical stuff, including kid problems, favorite television programs, our canine friends (both of our households had dogs), church, and school events. I'm sure they gossiped a bit as well. Both Denise and I played with Franny's kids, Boopsie (Mary Frances) and Joe.

Franny had a pleasant personality, a caring nature, and a smile bright enough to power a small country. She was a dynamic lady, short and stout, who had a huge, hearty laugh that resonated throughout our home. Franny was always there for us, meeting the moment's needs with a laugh and a smile and providing a reassuring and uplifting atmosphere just by her presence. With one daughter and two sons, she had plenty to keep her busy throughout the day; yet she still found time to help her neighbor.

Franny would always stop in to see if we needed anything or sometimes just to talk. She and my mom could share family stories, both well-told and brand new, and often did. Like her friend, my mother loved to engage in conversation. Sitting down with Franny over a cup of coffee and a Danish pastry provided precious moments for her to reminiscence, chuckle, and be her old self again.

As the years went by and mom's disease worsened, she was confined to a hospital bed in our living room. Franny made her dinner each night, delivering it on a tray with all the trimmings. She was an excellent cook who covered both Italian and Polish specialties. Mom's favorite dish was Beef Stroganoff. It's funny, but I didn't find out that Franny's husband, Ed, actually made the meal many years later. I couldn't understand Franny's motivation to provide food. Perhaps she sensed that the culinary skills of a fifteen-year-old boy weren't quite up to the task – or, God forbid, maybe she just smelled my cooking from next door.

When my mother died on September 16th, 1973, I knocked on Franny's door to tell her before I notified anyone else. She came over right away and helped me call some of my relatives.

As a kid, I saw people like Franny as angels on earth, special beings who love and care unconditionally, without strings or motivation. She saw a need and stepped up to make our lives easier. How lucky we were to have such a loving neighbor. But you just can't pay someone like this back in monetary terms.

I wanted to show her my appreciation throughout my life to let her know that a young boy recognized her contribution to my family through her selfless deeds. I started to visit her every Christmas Eve, not unlike Charles Dickens's ghosts, except that I brought glad tidings with me. Franny would greet me with a big kiss and a hug; then, before I had even sat down, she'd have a sandwich, potato chips, a soda, and some chocolate chip cookies in front of me. We would sit and laugh for a few hours as I updated her on my life's events.

She had moved from Southwest Philadelphia to Drexel Hill, but her home was still cozy, beautifully decorated, full of love, and warm as a toasty fireplace. And she always had a cat. Occasionally, though rarely, the feline would acknowledge me by rubbing against my leg and purring. Franny would smile brightly and tell me how unusual it was for the tabby to make a fuss over anybody.

The last time I saw Franny, I brought my wife, Donna, to meet her. On Christmas Eve of 1998, we had just come from visiting my father-in-law in Newtown Square. Donna's dad, Larry, was recovering from surgery in a rehabilitation facility, and Franny's house was on the way home for us. I'm so glad that Franny got to know that I had settled down. She always worried about me, wondering if I would weather life's storms without breaking. The small boy she used to refer to as Michael/Bikal had moved many times since we were next-door neighbors.

Those laughs and smiles we shared during that holiday visit came to mean the world to me. It was January 3, only days after our Christmas Eve visit, when I received a call from Franny's daughter, Boopsie, letting me know that her mother had died suddenly at 75 years of age. It was a gut-wrenching message to receive. I fought back the tears as she could barely hold on to her emotions through the call. I suddenly realized how lucky I was to see her over the Christmas holiday, especially since she got the chance to meet my wife.

I imagine that the minute Franny made it through the heavenly gates, she and my mother took a nice long walk among the clouds, sharing those family stories of old. And I picture Mom, no longer ill, sitting proudly at a dinner table alongside Franny as they critique the red sauce.

All is good!

12

My Scottish Grandmother

My dad's mom, Anne

The relationship between grandmothers and their grandchildren has been recognized by experts on family life as one of the few in which both parties are crazy about each other simply because they are there. To me, grandmothers are the best. This was the case with me and my dad's mother, Anne.

Grandmom had a lovely Scottish brogue, her accent so thick at times that I didn't always understand her. She often referred to me as Michael/son. Whenever the grandchildren went to her home, we would find candy and nuts stored in a fancy, decorated little bowl in every room in her apartment. And she had plenty of soda and potato chips on hand to please our childish palates.

She almost always wore housedresses in our presence but donned beautifully patterned dresses on special occasions and never cooked without an apron. Her hair, worn in a bun, was accentuated by long braids that she pulled up to wrap around her head. Kids who were lucky enough to sleep overnight at her place watched in amazement as she undid those braids and let her long, flowing gray hair down to brush it out before she went to bed. We all wondered how she managed to hide all that hair up top.

Grandmom was kind, sweet, astute, and wise. She would sit you down and explain things to you in a manner that you could understand unless, of course, the Scottish brogue got in the way. However, she wasn't much of a hugger until after she'd had a few beers. Then she would relax a little, gather the grandchildren around her, and sing "Danny Boy," enticing the kids to dance with her. She was most playful during this time and so much fun to be around.

My grandmother loved The National Enquirer, a tabloid newspaper that featured sensational headlines and stories meant to entertain rather than inform. She always had several issues stacked in the living room magazine rack. We, youngsters, got to marvel at who was "Marrying an Alien" or "The Pig that Ate Chicago." Even at that, I never figured out her fascination with those newspapers.

She also told fortunes. That is a well-known trait among the Scots. Her unique method of determining your fate was not by gazing into a crystal ball, examining your palm, or reading your tarot cards but by studying the suds that formed on the bottom of your empty beer glass. (Needless to say, none of us kids ever had our futures read, although I must admit that my grandmom and grandpop would let us take a sip from their glasses once in a while.)

Once I had a wart on the end of my left elbow, a spot that repeatedly banged into sturdy objects such as furniture, walls, and appliances. My grandmother took me aside and told me to rub a freshly cut potato onto the wart and then bury the potato in our backyard. I remember giving her the sideways doggy look, but she was serious. She guaranteed that the wart would disappear. I loved my grandmother, but I wasn't buying that one. Years later, I would lose the wart in a body-boxing match with a friend.

She kept her apartment spotless, the smell of Pine-Sol disinfectant filling the air. You could eat off her floors without fear. At one time or another, she also lived with just about everybody in the McCullough lineage, including in-laws and outlaws. She spent some time with our family when my mother became ill at thirty-seven years old. In fact, when I was twelve, she told me that I would have to learn how to cook, clean, iron, and do laundry. We didn't know much about multiple sclerosis at that point. No one did. But my grandmother's instincts were spot on as mom lost more ability by the day.

During that time, we had a dog named Sam. My mom drank a lot of coffee, at least ten cups daily. She made hers very strong. She always saved some for Sam – and she got him hooked. The poor dog had to quit cold turkey as he would not drink my grandmother's coffee brew. She was livid, stomping into the kitchen while Sam stuck his nose up and refused to touch it. Snookered, unaware that we harbored a caffeine-addicted dog, Grandmom would yell in that delightful brogue, "Sam, you pain in the ass." And he would defy her, barking into the early morning hours, his coffee nerves unserved.

My grandmother moved to Bartram Village, about a mile away from where most of my family lived. She so wanted to remain independent. Again, her apartment was small but beautiful. She supported herself by cleaning other homes during her lifetime, many of those on the Main Line in Philadelphia. She also cleaned offices in Center City. Grandmom never had it easy but continued to work in her later years.

On one occasion, dad, mom, and I drove down to pick my grandmother up at her apartment. We planned to have her over to our house for dinner that evening. It was a sweltering, hot summer day, and my father's automobile had no air conditioning. As we waited for her to come outside, another vehicle had parked at the end of her walkway. Not noticing our family waiting, she walked down the concrete sidewalk and opened the door to the auto sitting there. It was full of black folks, understandably startled when Grandmom tried to get into the back seat. We heard her say, in her delightful accent, "Oh, I'm sorry; you know I'm color blind." We overheard a hearty laugh coming from the open window in front of us.

Bless her heart, she was referring to the color of the car. She really couldn't tell green from purple or blue. So, we exited dad's sedan and introduced ourselves to the other people. We all laughed at the situation.

Her neighbors looked after my grandmother, which we so appreciated. Our biggest fear was how far she lived from our neighborhood. Accustomed to walking a block or two, at most, to reach all our relatives, we now had to cover more ground. Times were different in 1968. The Bartram Village apartment would be her last home.

Because of my mom's illness, the family used a concerted effort to keep the news of my grandmother's cancer battle from her. At eighteen years old, I should have been told, given she was very ill for six months, but I was my mom's caregiver most of the time. So, they kept the news from me, too. The family feared my mom wouldn't handle the news well since she was so close to her mother-in-law. Plus, mom was on powerful nerve medicine, whereby any sad information would leave her in a fragile state. Dad took me to the hospital to see my grandmother on the day she would pass, September 12, 1972, at sixty-seven years old. A year and four days later, my mom would join her.

I'm confident that my grandmother was a saint in her life, so I imagine God takes excellent care of her these days. In fact, I'm sure that she has candy and nuts placed into fancy, decorated little bowls located all over heaven.

13

Wedded Bliss

Aunt Cass and Uncle Dave

S omewhere in the mid to late 1950s, my Aunt Cass and Uncle Dave began to set up shop, having recently married and purchased a home on 61st Street between Elmwood and Grays Avenues.

Born on August 19, under the Zodiac sign of Leo, Aunt Cass lit up every room that she walked into. She reminded me somewhat of Debbie Reynolds, given her petite size, hair coloring, and attitude.

Fun-loving and engaging, Aunt Cass had the silliest of laughs. At any moment, she could giggle and, within mere seconds, have everyone laughing.

Soft-spoken and respectful, Uncle Dave would become my godfather when I came along. He had a kind, peaceful nature and an offbeat sense of humor. When my uncle told a joke, there was a slight wink in his eye, the wink usually directed at the kids. He always wanted us to get it. He loved country music, especially Johnny Cash songs, including his favorites, "Folsom Prison Blues" and "I Walk the Line," which didn't fit in with his newly minted in-laws. The McCullough family preferred the Big Band sounds of the 1940s.

Uncle Dave worked hard all his life. He became an excellent windshield and glass man for Jack's Auto Parts, located on 61st Street but closer to Passyunk Avenue by the river. (Many Southwest Philly residents will remember the used-parts places that took up a critical portion of 61st Street between Jerry's Corner and the 61st Drive-In Theater.)

My favorite story told by Uncle Dave concerned a fellow employee who one day called out sick. Uncle Dave was near the phone when it rang, so he answered it. The call went like this: "Dave, this is Horace; tell Herb (the owner) that I won't be in today. I had one of those epileptic fits." There was just one tiny glitch with this message. His co-worker didn't have epilepsy.

Uncle Dave spent many a day weathering the elements and enduring the lasting smells of lubricant, oil, and burning motors that permeated the shop where he worked. Besides the hideous odors, junkyard dogs guarded the whole area, roaming through the properties late into the evening, providing security for the auto parts owners. Those canines were every bit as mean as they have been portrayed. It is one thing for an unfamiliar pooch to approach you but quite another for a mangy-looking, maniacal hound to track you while you walked the property. Not only were these animals lying in grease all night, but their teeth appeared jagged and ominous, too, as if they chewed on old car batteries for fun.

Aunt Cass, always the proper wife, planned to have dinner on the table at 5:00 p.m. when Uncle Dave arrived home. Only one small problem stood in her way. Aunt Cass was also the adventurous one of the McCullough kids, who numbered four in total. (Mickey was the oldest, then Agnes, then Cass, and Johnny.) She hadn't hung around long enough to observe her mother's culinary skills, so this dinner-on-the-table stuff was a fresh experience for her.

To earn good graces with his mother-in-law, Uncle Dave would stop in to check on her each day before he would head home to his wife. He would stay for maybe twenty minutes to ensure that she was okay. Meanwhile, knowing her Scottish mom well, Aunt Cass assumed that she had fed her new husband a meal. Working on this assumption, Aunt Cass would have a wedge of cake, iced to the max, waiting for Uncle Dave when he arrived at the kitchen table.

My grandmother had not fed my uncle anything, but he was just too polite to tell my aunt. On Monday, she gave her new hubby a slice of pound cake. Tuesday's surprise was a chocolate torte. On Wednesday, she greeted my uncle with a piece of apple pie. By Thursday, poor Uncle Dave, now famished, had had enough and screamed, "Jesus Christ, Cass, I want some meat!"

Then there was the first time that Aunt Cass made pasta for her new spouse. In those days, they called it macaroni. She put the dried, long noodles into the pot and turned it on. Burning the hell out of spaghetti is quite the achievement. Being adventurous might have been one of Aunt Cass's admirable character traits; however, sometimes hanging around your mother while she's cooking pays dividends. For example, Aunt Cass might have noticed that you need to add water to the cooking vessel for this entire pasta thing to work.

In the end, Aunt Cass turned out to be a terrific cook. I had the pleasure of eating her homemade gravy with meatballs many times. Uncle Dave died on July 8, 1988, succumbing to congestive heart failure. Aunt Cass passed away silently into the morning on May 6, 2018, at the tender age of 86.

When my mother died in 1973, Aunt Cass proved invaluable in helping me to find my way over the first few weeks. She had me over to her house, and we would talk for hours, discussing the *whys* and *hows* of what happened to my mom. Years later, I would bring her over to our place, treating her to movies and dinner. She and I loved watching films together. One of the funniest times was viewing *Pearl Harbor* on my sixty-inch HDTV screen and 5.1 surround-sound system. A pivotal scene occurred at a train station where a few anxious airmen awaited the new nurses' arrival. The locomotive roared as it approached the depot. As the volume continually increased, the drywall shook as if the train would burst through at any second. I glanced over at my aunt. Her eyes were the size of dinner plates, her fear palpable. Unknowingly, I was sitting on the remote control wedged under a throw pillow next to me.

The memories are warm and funny and fond. I miss them both terribly and often wish they were still around.

That said, I hope that somehow, any time pasta is on the heavenly dinner menu, Uncle Dave gets a charge out of this memory, and Aunt Cass has the angels doubled over in laughter.

14

The Snowball

Bob Dougherty (Doc)

One cold winter day in 1966, the "young heads" took on the "old heads" in a snowball fight. It was a rite of passage that we up-and-comers welcomed to grab some street cred from these men on the path to marriage, having kids, growing beer bellies, and moving out to the suburbs.

I had the privilege of having a mature sister who stayed on friendly terms with many of the neighborhood's older dudes. The "old heads" I remember included Jake McGowan, Robert "Doc" Dougherty, Denny Mohan, Johnny McDade, Al Murphy, and Rich "Woody" Wood. Most of these guys were six to seven years older than we were. Our "young head" gang included Jack Mossman, Bubbles Davies, Bobby Cupps, and me.

To think that our side had a chance in this snowball battle was foolish. We were still growing into our bodies, some less quickly than others. I was a runt, but I had a temper, much like a scrappy pup. The "old heads," in their late teens, possessed more muscular arms and pinpoint accuracy. Their experience far outweighed ours, but we had enough spunk to think we could compete with these guys.

I remember ducking behind a parked station wagon to secure some cover and plan my next move. A short time later, from my seat on the curb behind the vehicle and my task of crafting a battle-worthy snowball, I stood up to check the area. Much to my surprise, Doc had me dead in his crosshairs, and it was too late to duck back down. He hit me in the nose with a snowball the size of a softball. I never saw him uncork the throw.

Fifty-three years later, I can still feel that snowball break over my nose like a wave, spreading over my cheeks and lips and collecting inside the curvature of my ears, where it came to a stop. It was a direct hit, totally without malice, just brilliantly aimed and powerfully thrown. My face stung for a second and then got numb as the icy crystals encircled my head. The sensation mimicked being punched with a 70 mile-per-hour snow cone, minus the sugary flavor. The toss, so powerful, knocked me flat on my ass.

Doc stood six feet, five inches tall. A strapping 225-pound redhead, he had pasty white skin speckled with thousands of freckles, all but guaranteeing dermatologist visits for the rest of his life unless he spread SPF-1000 suntan lotion over his body whenever he ventured out into the sunshine. His hands were the size of my head. The snowball that creased my skull was a good three to four pounds of tightly packed powdery snow and ice. Thank God that the temperature that day wasn't below twenty degrees; otherwise, Doc's roundish cold weapon would have frozen solid and killed me, leaving some other poor schmuck to tell this story.

It wasn't enough that Doc was a tall redhead who would score with the chicks, but the dude also had to have a howitzer for a throwing arm. He played first base because of his height, the baseball theory being that you needed the first baseman to be a big target, someone who can catch throws made too high and too wide for the average-sized guy. Doc was a natural there.

One day recently, I enjoyed talking with Doc; his wife, Helen, my friend, Mary Marker; my sister, Denise; and her husband, Denny. When I mentioned the snowball incident to Doc, he had no recollection of it, a common thing that happens when you age. Every stupid thing you've ever done in your life is suddenly forgiven as if your brain has built up too many dumb incidents, can't take it anymore, and paroles some of them as if they'd never happened. They escape at night through your snoring or get captured in your C-Pap mask for release into the atmosphere the following morning.

Three years after this snowball battle, Denny Mohan would marry my sister, Denise, and have Woody serve as his best man. I participated as an usher at my sister's wedding, almost resulting in my ex-communication from the Catholic Church. Let's just say that the confession of my sins to the priest didn't go very well. I received two rosaries as my penance that day.

We never know when we'll face our end. Despite having friends who served in the Vietnam War, the older guys have lost only Johnny McDade, who died of a heart ailment in the early 1990s. In our crew, only Jack Mossman and I remain. We lost Bubbles Davies on August 25, 1991, and Bobby Cupps in 2013 at the tender age of 59.

The six of us reminisced all through our meal. That good friends last a lifetime was evident that day. More than a few times, we mentioned how lucky we had been to have so many kids with whom to play in our old Southwest Philly neighborhood. And that's why fifty-three years later, we could sit, have a nice lunch, poke fun at each other, and laugh all afternoon.

Blessed are those folks who appreciate life's little pleasures. It really is that simple.

15

Bobby Cupps – Summer Tales

Bobby Cupps

I n 1968, at the age of fourteen, two buddies and I played catch on 2600 Robinson Street. In those days, as any Southwest Philly kid could tell you, the pimple ball ruled our lives. We used it to play stickball, wire ball, box ball, and wall ball through all hours of the day and into the night. The pimple ball was a white, soft, hollow rubber sphere filled with air equivalent in size to a tennis ball. Its unique cover was designed with small bumps or pimples to better grip it.

Today, we were long tossing, a technique defined as throwing a ball over considerable distances, increasing each interval gap. This practice helped to strengthen your arm. Bobby Cupps was standing at Latimer's property, while Jack Mossman and I stood in front of an elderly neighbor's household, a good one-hundred-seventy-feet away from Bobby. The older gentleman was pushing eighty-five. Concerned for his windows, he asked us if we could move a little farther up the street. We agreed, and Jack and I approached his front steps to apologize to him.

To reach the front door of any home on my block necessitated climbing two sets of steps. A flat landing was between these flights of steps where Jack and I stood as we approached our neighbor. He held his screen door wide open as he talked to us from his enclosed porch.

Meanwhile, Bobby had the ball, waiting for us to return to our position in the street. As he was apt to do, he soon grew impatient and unleashed a laser toss in our direction. He had an arm like Hall of Famer Roberto Clemente, and his throw struck the bottom aluminum panel of the man's exterior metal door.

Bobby must have hit it dead center. The deafening noise startled the elderly man, so much so that he fell backward into his enclosed porch. Jack and I stood there in consternation, hoping with all our might that we hadn't caused him to have a heart attack and not knowing in the slightest what to do. Just then, Bobby's infectious laugh carried all the way down the street. Helpless, Jack and I broke into laughter, too, and took off running. I felt terrible. This neighbor was such a nice man; I literally wanted to crawl into a hole and die. How could I face him now each and every day as I walked by his property?

These and other such situations with our feisty friend kept us jumpy. We had to watch him like a hawk. He often rang doorbells, lit fires, and caused other havoc. To him, those activities defined the word "fun." To me, they described the term "mayhem."

One day I borrowed my sister's bicycle. On the way up the street, I ran into Bobby, and we went to the Cellar Store at 61st Street and Elmwood Avenue to buy some candy. A typical girl's two-wheeler, my sister's bike had no cross-piece to carry a passenger. (A boy's bike had a metal pipe or crossbar that connected the frame beneath the handlebar assembly to the seat support, enabling someone small to sit on the bar without restricting the rider's ability to pedal or steer the cycle.) Bobby was at least four inches taller than I was, so he rode the bike while I sat on the handlebars, a far riskier prospect for both travelers as the rider had to deal with the additional weight of his passenger balancing on the steering wheel.

It was a stifling hot summer day. As we left the store to go home, I again mounted the handlebars while Bobby pedaled and steered the bike. Sixty-First Street, at the corner of Elmwood Avenue, was the high point of the block. It was all downhill towards Buist Avenue. We took off as if we really knew what we were doing.

Bobby was a speed demon and a pure sports car enthusiast. Why I didn't think this through escapes me. We picked up momentum, the warm breeze blowing against our faces. The bike was flying as we approached the Firmani household, three-quarters of the way down the block and at least one hundred feet before our Buist Avenue destination.

Suddenly, Bobby lost control, and we crashed into a parked plumber's truck. On impact, a jolting thud echoed the sound of a bike tire meeting the rear metal bumper. Launched off the handlebars like a rocket, I hit the back door with my head. The bicycle bounced back off the vehicle, dragging Bobby as it spun circles on the asphalt before coming to a stop. If that wasn't scary enough, a loud, piercing scream followed as two women witnessed a kid flying through the air and a bike bending out of shape in front of them. The women, who'd been sitting on their porches nearby, rushed down to help.

As I peeled my body off the truck, I saw that Bobby had cut both his right knee and ear. He was bleeding, and the women reacted as if someone had shot him with a gun. They picked him up and brought him into the house to dress his wounds and give him some ice cream. Had soft music, blankets, and hot-water bottles followed, I wouldn't have been surprised.

Meanwhile, Concussion Boy, who had made a direct hit on the truck with his face, received little to no attention. It must have been because I wasn't bleeding – forget that I saw multitudes of sparkling lights flashing before my eyes and thought that our current President was Abe Lincoln. The women abandoned me, leaving me on the ground to ponder the fact that I was alive doubtless only because of the thickness of my inherited Scots Irish skull.

Slowly and painfully, I wrestled my sister's bike up off the ground. The frame was bent so much so that the wheels wouldn't turn. Although I lived only a block away, it would still be a long walk home, dragging that bike with me. While Bobby enjoyed the tender loving care of his attentive nurses, I was faced with having to explain to my older sister why she couldn't ride her bicycle anymore.

16

A Southwest Philly Christmas

Me and my drums

The Christmas season in Southwest Philly was a magical time of the year. Homes were adorned with holiday decorations on each block, and Christmas lights shone so bright it looked as if nighttime would never come. The bulbs that hung on the exterior of the houses were big and multicolored, unlike the white light displays you notice today. Although the modern lighting arrangements are exquisite, they lose their charm when it looks as if teams of workers dropped by to do the decorating. I don't see the neighbors climbing ladders, reaching out to their front windows, or getting on the roof anymore. And of course, as you get older, the task becomes more difficult to do.

Back then, trees got decorated much closer to the Christmas holiday. Some families would often wait until Christmas Eve when the price of the trees had dropped to a more reasonable level. I remember putting up our tree as late as Christmas Eve one time. I'm guessing that mom paid less than five bucks that year. Today we hang the decorations right after Thanksgiving. To my way of thinking, the earlier I decorate, the more time I have to relax and enjoy the festivities.

As a tradition, we always left our ornaments hung until Little Christmas, which falls on January 6. We still do. Other folks toss their trees in the dumpster a few days after Christmas. The festive atmosphere was present everywhere we went. On Woodland Avenue, store owners and local committee groups decorated our shopping area for blocks, hanging garland, wreaths, and lights. The sounds of the season played late into the night, almost everywhere, as you walked along the avenue. You could buy fresh Christmas trees on the pavements from large, burly, bundled-up men who kept warm standing around open fires housed in rusty metal trash cans. (It makes me wonder if our weather was much colder in those times.) The smell of the fresh trees combined with the improvised ash-can fire pits generated an odor instantly recognizable in an urban setting.

Southwest Philly, however, was a neighborhood that had everything. Woodland Avenue was home to a few sizable retail stores. Murphy's, Jupiter's, Woolworth's, and John's Bargain Store existed along with compact specialty shops like Bob White's, Jay's Army & Navy, Chernoff, and Kovnat's. The avenue also included a couple of banks, a credit union, two supermarkets, and two small restaurants.

I remember walking down to 66th and Woodland, where an appliance business had a color TV on display in the window. It intrigued me, so I would stop by and stare at it for a half-hour. If your television had color in the 1960s, you were doing well. And what teenager didn't spend an afternoon and an allowance in Jolly's Records? I bought my first 45 rpm record there, "Glad All Over," by the Dave Clark Five. Then there was Centrella's, where rotisserie chickens were turning crispy right in front of you. If you wanted to meet their still-feathered relatives, you had only to go inside where you would find Cousin George or Mary Sue making all kinds of racket in their cages.

There were so many Catholics living in the area. We enjoyed an abundance of religious activities to go along with the commercial aspect of the holiday. On my block, our neighbor Carmen Peca's Christmas hymns echoed through the night on speakers he had attached to the front walls of his second floor. He was a quiet guy who preferred playing instrumental songs rather than the more popular Bing Crosby or Brenda Lee hits of the day. I always loved hearing those Christmas carols. We would play touch football on the street as the sound of "Silver Bells" reminded us of the holidays and days off that were approaching. And if by chance it snowed, the world around us became magical. Having music, lights, and snow during the Christmas season was indeed a kid's blessing.

January 6 marked the religious end of the season. People took the fresh Christmas trees to the big park between 2600 Robinson and

Dewey Streets. The older teenagers, or "old heads," as we called them, would scour the neighborhood for those real trees, collect them, and bring them to the open grounds. They would put the trees in the center of the field stacked high into the sky. After the crowd would gather around, they would set the pile ablaze like a massive Viking funeral celebration. While the lighter load made the trash collectors happy, I'm pretty sure that the fire department didn't smile that day. However, the park was so spacious that there was no danger to the existing homes.

When the New Year arrived, the magic dissipated, leaving us to face the cold reality of winter weather. With the ornamentation and lights removed, the anticipation, glee, and excitement of the season now sat unused, tied up, boxed, bagged, and put away for eleven months. Yet to this day, I never fail to be amazed at how some festive lighting, decorations, and Christmas spirit uplifts everyone. I wish the rest of the year could be this charming.

17

A Double Dose Of Bubbles (Bobby Davies)

Bubbles

The year was 1970. It was one of those nights when we couldn't get warm. Getting enough guys to play some touch football failed us; it was just too cold. Bobby "Bubbles" Davies' father had a comfortable four-door sedan, and luckily, he had time off from work that evening. Bubbles, Bobby B., and I took shelter in Mr. Davies' automobile to escape the biting wind. He had parked the Chevy on 2600 Robinson Street in front of his next-door neighbor's home. Bubbles sat in the driver's seat while Bobby occupied the passenger side. I sat alone in the backseat, unaware of what was about to happen.

I guess we were in there for about a half-hour when I noticed the two of them giggling, hands to mouths preventing me from hearing what they were talking about. I leaned forward and placed my head on the back of the front seat (two-seaters weren't standard then). I heard Bobby B. laughing, so I looked in his direction on the car's passenger side. In an instant, I saw a bright flash. He hit me right between the eyes with tear gas fired from a gun or a smaller cartridge-type pistol. The tear gas spread throughout the automobile with a smothering effect. I couldn't see anything. Covering my face as best I could, I tried desperately to find my way out of the car, blindly reaching for a handle while pushing my shoulder into the door. I fell onto Robinson Street, rolling across the asphalt and up over the curb to the lawn where the Stinger's lived. The burning sensation intensified with each passing second. I kept rubbing my sweater into my eye sockets to stop the searing pain. I discovered later on that covering your eyeballs was the worst thing to do in that situation.

Bobby B., meanwhile, had escaped the smoke-filled vehicle and ran up the street. Dopey Bubbles had totally forgotten that his father's auto had a hole in the floor on the driver's side of the car. He was in such a hurry to get out that his foot caught in the six-inch opening just underneath him. He was trapped in the automobile with all the tear gas. I would say that justice was served on the spot, but the shooter got away scot-free, with no trace of tear gas on his person. The kid who split didn't recognize or understand the danger of what he did that night.

My eyes cleared up in about a half-hour. I was so relieved, considering the possibility that this stupidity might have blinded me. As a working welder, I know now that our eyes can take a lot of punishment, but this episode truly scared me. Although Bubbles survived to fight another day, I'm sure that his dad freaked out when he had to drive to work the following day. Who knows how long tear gas hangs around once it has penetrated seat material and rugs? To be honest, Bobby B. struggled with logic, so there was no telling how all this affected him.

I can't answer for Bobby B., and sadly, Bubbles died at a young age. I never found out what instrument he used to shoot me to this day. In fact, this happened so many years ago that I still don't remember how we resolved the issue, whether we argued or fought over it. The main point is how stupid and irresponsible we were.

I did gain a new respect for tear gas. It is as nasty as you think it is. I didn't qualify for military service, so I never got to partake in tests the recruits go through in basic training to expose them to toxic elements for the first time. I understand that the trainees enter a room containing the poisonous fumes wearing a full-face respirator to protect them. They have to remove the protective mask to feel the actual effect of the tear gas and get timed by how long they can tolerate the smoke. I'm guessing that my experience was similar except for the shock value of being hit directly in the face with it.

I imagine that an angel must have been sitting on my shoulder that night. To have no permanent damage done to my eyes was nothing short of a miracle, considering that I had been shot at point-blank range. And sometimes, it's just the luck of the Irish. Either way, I'll take it.

Let's fast forward twelve years to 1982. On a long, hot summer evening, I attended a Phillies game. My girlfriend had partial-season tickets for the home games, but she'd gone away with her parents on vacation. So, I brought my friend Johnny Nace to the event, and although the Phillies won that night, the heat and humidity were unbearable. It's miserable when you sit in a crowded stadium with no breeze. Plus, you're close enough to the guy next to you to touch your knees. After the ballgame ended, I dropped Johnny off and headed home, hoping to get some sleep. The following morning at the Navy Yard, I had to work an overtime day, a rare occasion for me.

In those days, I lived above a store at 62nd Street and Buist Avenue. I shared a two-story apartment with a couple of friends. We had no air conditioning. I took a shower to cool off and headed to my small bedroom on the third floor. As I lay in bed that night, I wished and hoped that the window shade would swing out and in, anything showing some movement. I needed assurance that there would be a breeze. However, it was not to be. My window curtain moved with all the speed of a twelve-day-old corpse. I couldn't sleep or relax, and the hours eroded away a minute at a time. The desk clock neared the time of 2:00 a.m., and I still couldn't close my eyes even with the knowledge that I needed to get up at 6:00 a.m. for work.

As I tossed and turned fitfully, I heard the telephone ring. *Oh, my God,* I thought, *it's 2:30 in the morning. Who's calling me at this hour?* I jumped out of bed and proceeded to the second floor to answer the phone. Now the caller asked me to guess his name. If the heat were not sufficiently torturing me already, I now had some goofball breaking my balls to identify him.

After a minute, I blurted out, "Enough; who the hell is this?" The guy answered, "It's Bubbles, you dumbass." Instantly I brightened up and asked, "Bubbles, where are you?"

He told me that he was at Anne Mossman's house.

"I'll be there in a few minutes," I said. And just that quickly, I was heading out to visit an old friend whom I hadn't seen in a decade or more.

We had a blast that night. Bubbles and his sister, Lisa, were at Anne's house, and we must have drunk and laughed for three hours. I was so glad to be in his company that I almost forgot about needing to be at work on hardly any sleep. Bubbles, Jack Mossman, and I had hung out for a few years, playing touch football and learning to drink alcohol, rites of passage that almost every teenage boy goes through as part of his maturing. Along the way, we had developed a bond and a unique friendship that I still cherish all these years later.

As the cock crowed and the sun rose, we said our goodbyes. I had no way of knowing that it was the last time I would ever see Bubbles. But sadly, it was, as he died on August 25, 1991. I have always been thankful that I answered the phone that night, for those memories have stayed with me forever. Those final moments and the circumstances of our get-together make me smile. It was a treat to spend quality time with him and Lisa again.

When I wrote this story, I had just attended Anne Mossman Cook's funeral. It was at her house that Bubbles and I last met. Anne also died way too young. My point in writing it was —and is – that it's critical to let your friends and families know how you feel about them because not one of us is guaranteed tomorrow.

18

Wild, Wild, Wildwood Days

Aunt Mary, John-John, Uncle John

The year was 1967. My Aunt Aggie and Uncle Vince owned a summer property in Wildwood, New Jersey. It was a three-story house with a separate bungalow in the backyard, so there were plenty of places to stash relatives, wanted or not. My mom and I used to go down for a two-week vacation while dad stayed home. A triple-dipper, he despised the shore, disliked the sun, and hated the sand. (His loss!) Thankfully, my dad's brother, Johnny, drove Aunt Cass, my mother, cousins Anne and Cassie, and me to Wildwood. We had a crowded carload. Uncle John's wife, Mary, would arrive with their son, John-John, the following day.

On this day from our past, Uncle John would set a modern-day record for how long it took to drive to Wildwood from Philadelphia. The ride lasted for four hours. To be honest, I thought that he was the coolest uncle I had, only fourteen years my senior. However, my uncle did not handle stress well. Missing Exit 7S on the Garden State Parkway and taking Exit 7N instead placed him heading north to the wrong beaches. Driving with a vehicle full of kids is no easy walk in the park at the best times, and it gets worse when they sing.

At the height of his miserable trip, I remember hearing the tune "Surfin' Bird," also called "The Bird is the Word," by The Trashmen. It was a novelty song with repetitive lyrics that had caught fire that summer. It sounded something like this: "Bird, bird, bird, well, the bird is the word, I said the bird, bird, bird, the bird's the word." It was annoying beyond comprehension, performed by a guy whose vocals suggested that his throat required immediate medical attention. The nephew and nieces sang the hit record at the top of their lungs to complicate the situation further. To appreciate my uncle's futility, go to YouTube and listen to this music.

Meanwhile, Uncle John, lost, confused, and now aggravated, was operating a non-air-conditioned car. I recall that he almost drove off the highway before pulling over to the side of the road, where we all exited the automobile for a much-needed break.

Once we arrived in town, though, everything went fine. My aunt's house provided plenty of room for all the guests. Mom and Aunt Cass stayed on the second level with my two cousins and me.

Uncle John's clan had the bungalow all to themselves. Aunt Aggie, Uncle Vince, and their five little buggers, Kathy, Vincy, Kevin, Anne, and Monica, were on the first floor. We all had a blast when together. Vincy and I used to spend the entire day at the beach. We would go home, shower, eat, and then take a hike to the boardwalk at night. Back then, we were each given $2.50 to entertain ourselves. With that small amount of money, Vincy and I played miniature golf and rode the bumping cars. Then we had a slice of Mack's yummy cheese pizza along with their famous root beer soda, iced to the max. Without a Twin Kiss, no night would be complete. How could anyone resist this silky-smooth combination of vanilla and chocolate custard poured into a crispy cone with two chambers? We could stroll the boards from the Fun Pier near the entry to Wildwood Crest to the Sportland Pier at the other end into North Wildwood, ending at 17th Street. It was a three-mile trip, one way.

The boardwalk offered an extensive array of choices, all set to the classic rock soundtrack playing day and night. Guys and gals sold tie-dyed T-shirts. There were booths with board games, spinning wheels, batting cages, horse races powered by water pistols, and softball tosses at steel bottles. Vendors would guess your weight, and machines would clock your fastball speed. The enticing scents of pizza, popcorn, french fries, Italian sausages, kielbasa, and fudge wafted from the shops. The screams from the roller coasters were so loud that they could be heard for blocks. These amusement rides gave Wildwood a different vibe from the quieter shore towns such as Avalon, Stone Harbor, Sea Isle. Even though all the other vacation destinations had their unique spin on family fun, Wildwood had the most to do for everyone, especially the kids.

I remember how well I slept down at the shore. We didn't wear sunscreen in the1960s. In fact, Coppertone was the only product I recall. Because of my pasty white, Scottish skin coloring, I got sunburned so severely the walk after 7:00 p.m. would always bring chills. I wore a light jacket because the air was crisp from the sea breeze. In those days, the high tide took the water close to the boardwalk in the evening, enough that the sand under it remained damp the next day. (On that same beach today, because of ongoing erosion, children must deal with Gobi Desert conditions as they scramble, skip and jump at least two blocks before they reach the waves, trying desperately to keep their feet from getting burned.) When Vince and I arrived home, we played cards, had some snacks, and then hit the bed. Under the covers, I sensed the heat escaping my body and radiating through the thin top sheet. Combined with the soft ocean wind blowing over me, the soothing sensation put me to sleep until morning.

Looking back over the years, spending summer days in Wildwood was the time of our lives. For a week or two, depending on finances, we Southwest Philly kids could escape the hot summer streets filled with open fireplugs, the cries of fruit and vegetable hucksters, and mosquito trucks squirting chemicals into the air. Instead, we had only to wake up, eat some breakfast, then head for the ice-cold waters, where body surfing became our biggest sport. Rising up in a wave and crashing down, having no idea where our bodies would end up, became a gamble like no other: Would we make it to the beach in one piece, or be tossed around like rag dolls, tumbling over and over and driven into the ocean's shell-strewn bottom?

The anticipation began even before the instant that we caught the ocean air's salty smell as we crossed over the bridges into Wildwood. While the warmth of the sun and invigorating breezes found many spread along the beach, echoing throughout the day were the laughs and squeals of delighted children as bumping cars, an enormous Ferris Wheel, and the Tilt-a-Whirl rumbled away. I can still hear the beach-walking ice cream vendor shouting, "Fudgy Wudgy!" and sending young kids scampering after their parents to beg for money for some sugary treats. As I recall it, I am a boy again, waiting for the Wild Mouse to run downhill, yelling, hands in the air, as happy as a boy can get.

19

The 61ˢᵗ Street Drive-In

The old sign remained for years

As kids, we used to walk down to the 61st Street Drive-In during the summer months and sneak in through the fence. The oldest boy in our group was eleven years old, so none of us could drive cars, let alone own them. However, this majestic, outdoor, big-screen theater had a flaw that allowed us to take in a movie for free. There were illegal seats placed in the area just ahead of Row 1 in the parking lot. Someone had cut a large hole in the perimeter fencing and taken the time to put an old, beat-up couch on the premises.

The main drawback to this setup was our inability to hear the film, as we could never get close enough to hook up a speaker. Not to mention that we ran the risk of getting run over by a vehicle operated by a driver who had no clue that a sofa had been placed near the parking area! Everything was fine until we realized how many rats hung out at this venue, mainly to feast on all the popcorn, candy, and hot dog rolls that fell to the asphalt near the vehicles.

Drive-ins were fun but also a little creepy. One time, we watched the featured flicks from outside the property, standing on a railroad overpass that had a great view of the massive screen. Someone complained about being hungry, but none of us had any money. Then I remembered that we had cookies at my house. Everybody swooned at the mere mention, so off I went to steal the family treats.

Along with me for the walk was Jack Mossman. It would take a half-hour to return to our spot over top of the road if we had done that. Mischievous activity interrupted our plan. Two of our friends (I won't mention their names; let's just say they were the firebug twins) lit a bonfire in the dumps. Jack and I were about halfway back when suddenly, this massive fire developed right in front of us.

We did the smart thing and ran like crazy across 61st Street to the other side. We still had the cookies. We figured the cops or firefighters were already on the way. Why chance getting caught and allowing the police to end up with our treats? (This is the kid version of what happens when law enforcement runs the older guys off the corner and steals their beers.)

So Jack and I took off running, heading towards 63rd Street, where we would make our escape unscathed. But running through the dumps at night without a flashlight is roughly akin to running through a minefield. I don't know how many times I fell or ran into something. The area also used to have spots where bamboo stuck out of the ground. It made me wonder if we'd been beamed over to the Philippines. We braved it until exiting at 63rd Street and Lindbergh Boulevard. Incredibly, our sweet, crunchy snacks survived. Getting back to a previous analogy, men never drop their beer no matter the circumstances – and kids never let go of their delicious treats, either.

Of course, I still had to go home and play dumb about the missing chocolate chips. As a Catholic schoolboy, I already had a natural guilty look on my face. My parents saw right through my charade, and they punished me. To this day, I still feel ashamed even when I've done nothing wrong. What had those blue-robed indoctrinators done to us?

As I reminisce, I long for the time when the Drive-In offered its dollar-a-carload specials. These smart deals usually occurred in the middle of the week when the theater had fewer moviegoers. If you could fit six individuals in one car, you paid a buck. Otherwise, you might see people spilling out of the car's trunk to avoid paying the entry fee. We always had a good laugh over this, considering the cleanliness of a typical car trunk, having oil cans, greasy rags, extra tires, and other such debris taking up space.

I'm trying to imagine today's culture handling surprises as they drove down 61st Street. Anyone my age will remember those triple features at the drive-in. First up would be a war movie such as *Hell Is for Heroes*, starring Steve McQueen, followed by *Pillow Talk*, with Rock Hudson and Doris Day. The third feature would always be controversial, for example, an offering such as *Beyond the Valley of the Dolls*, a bottom-feeder-grade-B film featuring unknown actors, rampant nudity, no plot, no script, wild wigs, drugs, hippies, musicians, and outrageous outfits.

And here you were, a young Catholic boy coming home from South Philly after spending a night at grandma's apartment, with both parents in the car, passing by the drive-in just as an orgy was taking place on the screen in clear view from the road.

God, I miss those days.

20

Losing A Friend

Bobby Cupps

One night, on a whim, I felt the need to check on my sister, Denise. I hadn't been over to her house in a few weeks, which was unusual. I wanted to schedule a dinner out with Denise and her husband, Den. On arrival, I found my sister sitting in the family room. She looked at me curiously and asked me if I knew a Bobby Cupps. I said, "Sure; what's up?"

"Mary Marker told me that he died," she replied. Apparently, the day before, Denise and some of her old Southwest Philly friends had been out to lunch. During their meal, Mary had mentioned that her neighbor, Bobby Cupps, had passed away the previous day – January 16, 2013 – from cancer. I stood there, mouth agape, hit with a punch I had never seen coming, wondering what had happened to my childhood friend.

Bobby and I had lost touch some twenty years earlier. I didn't know where he lived now or how his life was going. His sister Donna had only recently told me something I'd never known about him. Before moving to our neighborhood in Southwest Philly, Bobby had been hit by a car while riding a bicycle. He was only six years old. On impact, his little body had been tossed high into the air before landing on the vehicle that hit him and then tumbling onto the street. Both speed and alcohol were involved in the accident, which occurred in broad daylight. Although the driver remained at the scene, it is unknown if any charges were filed against him.

A traumatic head injury left Bobby with epilepsy and compromised his ability to read, and he'd worn a body cast for six months. The doctors had not expected him to live, but Bobby had endured the ordeal and worked very hard to get better. For his injuries, he received a meager $1,500, held in trust until he turned 21. He hid his disability from the world, and I had to admire his resolve to go on living his life without complaint.

My friend Jack Mossman and I had always seen Bobby as one of the gang, no different from anyone else. He was athletic, strong, and fast. He was also engaging and quite the prankster. However, while Jack and I had attended a Catholic grade school, Bobby had gone to public school, so we'd never witnessed the struggles he went through to learn. He had the proverbial patience of a saint and enough mechanical skills to make a living. He was great at communicating with both kids and older folks. All that said, through all the mischief we'd gotten into, we had also come to regard Bobby as a wild child, a hyperactive kid, someone for whom we needed to keep an eye out. Now it all made sense.

I called Jack, who was as shocked as I'd been by the news, and we found out where his funeral was being held. I hooked up my GPS, and we headed to Easton, PA, a place that was totally unfamiliar to both of us. After a two-hour ride, we found the funeral parlor. Bobby's sister, Donna, and brother, Billy, stood by his casket with their mom, Marge. They were thrilled that we had come, having not seen either of us for such a long time.

Standing there, I couldn't help but think of the fun times we had had. Bobby, Jack, and I had shared many interests, including baseball and football. We'd had snowball fights, rung doorbells, and ran away (otherwise known as "Ding Dong Ditch," depending on what part of the neighborhood you grew up in) and generally created a bit more than our share of havoc. We'd all lived near each other, Bobby and Jack on the 2600 block of Dewey Street; I on the 2600 block of Robinson Street.

Bobby's hero was Elvis Presley, not only a charismatic singer but also an early advocate of using judo and other Asian self-defense methods in his motion pictures. Bobby hated school but had mastered these martial arts techniques with minimal effort. One day an argument we were having about a trivial matter morphed into a physical battle. Practice dummy Mike got flipped over Mr. Scott's hedges, trash cans, a parked car, and a sleeping dog before it ended. We made enough noise that my dad walked up the street to break it up. For whatever reason, he had never intruded on any of my activities before this. He told us to stop, shake hands, and apologize to each other, which we did. We were playing just fine later that afternoon.

On another afternoon, while hanging out in Jack's backyard, we created a new game. The idea was to throw darts out the second-floor bedroom window at targets placed around the lawn. As sometimes happens, life provides unexpected dark humor to the proceedings. How else to explain that I was impaled by a dart? Being trapped on Jack's grass with a bright, yellow projectile sticking out of my foot had not been a part of the plan.

You'd think that when a sharp object penetrates your body, your normal response would be to yank out the tiny spear. That's not what I did: I froze. I still remember Jack's grandmother screaming in her horrible scratchy voice as she removed the arrow from my instep. We were used to her yelling at us; she often did. I didn't even get a tetanus shot. I avoided that needle by not telling my parents. If I got disciplined at school, I never told mom or dad, either.

The dumps began on Eastwick Avenue's southern side in our neighborhood, covering a nine-block area that stretched from 61st to 70th Street. Railroad tracks existed to deliver essentials to local factories like Ryerson Steel and U.S. Gypsum. At the Eastwick Avenue/62nd Street intersection, a paved roadway ran from the street level down to the landfill base, a thirty-foot drop. The ramp was built to enable trucks to enter and exit the junkyard below. A wall stood on the southern portion of the driveway for safety. We boys had a lot of fun exploring the dumps in those days, playing for hours on end, inventing games as we went along.

Playing one spring day at the dumps, Jack and Bobby discovered these neat-looking wooden boxes that resembled tiny cages. Like women coming upon a great sale, we brought them home. What they'd found were animal traps designed for the tinier game, such as rabbits or squirrels. I imagine that a close neighbor was eating or selling the little critters. As one might expect, the guys who owned the contraptions tracked us down and retrieved their goods. How did we know we were messing with a family's food source or some young entrepreneur's new business?

We used to play at the dumps in wintertime, too. One cold morning we awoke to six inches of fresh snow, the perfect scenario for sledding. As I arrived at the site that day, I tested the slope to see how fast my sled would move. I was excited. Slick and icy, the surface looked like someone had sneaked in there during the night and sprayed the ramp with cold water. I looked up to the top of the hill, eager to make the next run. As I climbed laboriously up to the starting point, a sled, heading downward, just missed me.

Geared up with gloves, boots, and a knit cap, I waited for my chance to take off. My sled was old, with rusty rails and suspect durability. I took a running start, aimed at finding the quickest part of the course. About one-fourth of the way down, Bobby, coming up the ramp, leaped onto my back, landing square on the upper half of my torso. As he gleefully rode me down the unforgiving path, he completely blocked my view of the hill or anything else. Steering became increasingly problematic.

Laughing like a maniac, neither he nor I saw the opening in the wall. Halfway down the hill, the barrier had an eight-foot-wide break. We flew right through the gap, like Olympic ski jumpers, landing on a snow-covered abandoned automobile about ten feet below us at the bottom of the dumps.

We both were ejected from the sled but miraculously received no cuts or bruises. Bobby and I rolled over, laughing hysterically at our mishap. I picked up the mangled sled, cleaned myself off, and went to help Bobby get up. My already compromised sled had seen its last trip that day. Looking a slight bit red-faced, up the hill we went. It was just another adventuresome day in Southwest Philly.

Bobby's vital presence is one that I keenly miss. I would not put it past him even to sneak into the secure area to lock the Pearly Gates, just to keep Saint Peter engaged. A betting man would tell you, though, that he is in heaven raising holy hell, screaming for his Philadelphia Eagles, ringing the saintly residents' doorbells, and running away.

21

A Southwest Philly Treasure

Johnny McDade

J ohnny McDade was a Southwest Philly guy. He lived on the 2600 block of 62nd Street, on the other side of the alley from our house on Robinson Street. Like many of us, he attended St. Barney's and West Catholic but was a few years older than me and reflected more the age of my sister's crowd.

I always considered John one of my mother's special angels. She suffered from Multiple Sclerosis, robbing her of the ability to walk and eventually confining her to a hospital bed in our living room until her death at age forty-four. Johnny visited our home often and would do those tasks a stubborn twelve-year-old was not ready for: washing windows or laundering and hanging curtains and draperies. I did my best to keep up with the regular house chores, but John did these technical, time-consuming duties with the expertise of a cleaning company – and with a big smile on his face, too.

The youngest in his family, John, had five other siblings. He had a lot of experience helping his mother clean and maintain their home when she became ill. His mother was in poor health before my mom got sick. All this tedious stuff came easily to him. Thankfully for his mom, John stepped right up when his older brothers and sister married and left home.

A pleasant guy with boundless energy, he was a lifelong Eagles, Phillies, and Flyer's fan. However, as much as he loved his sports, he wasn't a natural athlete. In fact, his older sister Cathy reminded me that John was a klutz. He worked hard, hustled, and played with emotion but, always an unlucky sort, he would jump into a football scrum to help a friend and end up having his face spiked, necessitating a trip to the hospital for stitches to close the wound.

Because of his thoughtful and generous nature, we all thought of John as "a good egg." While in the Army, he asked my sister Denise if she would mind writing letters to two soldiers who never got mail. He always felt sorry for them. Denise obliged. (My sibling is a kind and generous person, too.)

At eighteen, Johnny sold me his 1964 Rambler for fifty dollars. I loved that car, even if it did sometimes stop on its own. Whenever the automobile changed gears from first to second, the auto would screech and come to a halt. This typically occurred while climbing a hill. It never happened while driving on a flat surface. We never figured it out, but it was okay as long as I went over 30 mph. I did not mention this strange quirk to John because I didn't want to embarrass him or seem ungrateful, given the meager cost of the vehicle.

For Christmas in 1970, John surprised me with my first pair of genuine ice hockey gloves, bought at a popular sports outlet in Center City. It thrilled me to receive this gift; at last, my equipment looked legitimate.

I used to visit all my mother's special angels on Christmas Eve, going to Franny Kusner's house first, Dot Bateman's second, and Johnny's last. He and his mom liked to stay up and watch the holiday specials. We would get caught up while John and his mother had a late-night sweet treat and some coffee. They always gave me some cold soda with ice. I helped with the dessert, but the next cup of java I drink will be my first.

After John's mom passed, I continued my yearly visits until he became a little hard to find during the holidays. Sometimes he flew out to California to visit his good buds Sally and Al Murphy, also Southwest Philly neighbors. Al Murphy and John were close friends, and Al's wife, Sally O'Hara, was my sister's best friend. One Christmas, John had convinced Al and Sally that he was sending them a Fed-Ex package on a date in 1988. It was close to the holiday, and still, nothing had arrived. When Sally and Al got home, they opened the blinds and saw Sally's mother sitting on their back patio furniture. John was hiding in the backyard. This was John's Christmas surprise to his friends as he had paid for both of their flights from Philadelphia. John was just that kind of a guy.

In previous years, both John and Al played softball and football with the corner gang, which included Jake McGowan, Jimmy Hartey, Anthony "Frog" Medaglia, Rich "Woody" Wood, Jackie O'Donnell, "Big" Bob Dougherty, and my brother-in-law, Denny Mohan.

John would leave this earth at the tender age of 47. I had stopped at his house that Christmas Eve but found that the lights were off. I'd forgotten that it was a year when he had flown out to California. I was painting my entryway at around 8 pm on a Friday in early January when our phone rang. It was my sister, Denise, informing me of his death. He had died peacefully in his sleep during the Christmas holiday at Murph and Sally's home. Thankfully, he had never suffered. I sat on the stairs for a long time pondering his passing, wondering how death could come so soon to somebody so young, so energetic, so full of life.

We all know people who put others' needs before their own. John was one of my mother's special angels who came along when we were really in need. He was a tremendous help to me, and I never forgot that. I believe that he's in heaven right now, sleeves rolled up, cleaning curtains. And, on the occasional football scrum, John jumps in to help a teammate, has his cheek spiked, and gets pain-free stitches for his efforts from that heavenly M.D., Saint Luke.

22

A Day With Sister Laura – Sixth Grade

A modern version of our classroom taken ten years ago

The year was 1966. Until the seventh grade, the nuns and teachers switched classes during the daytime while the children remained in the same room for seven hours. During one of these switches, we ran into an issue. Our homeroom instructor, Sister Laura, had finished teaching another class right before lunchtime. I don't remember who taught our session, but the nun or lay teacher had left our area to return to her regular part of the building.

As any kindergarten to a college-level teacher can tell you, leaving sixty students idle in a classroom is *never* a good idea. With no leader in place and accounted for, we couldn't be trusted. Any short period of unsupervised time allowed us to have fun and get into some trouble. I forget the particular havoc we wreaked that day, but we weren't behaving like good young Catholic men. I'm sure Sister Laura would have preferred silent reflection, maybe some meditation, a little catechism debate, or saying prayers while we awaited her return. But that didn't happen with 12-year-old boys in the 1960s or, I think it's safe to say, at any other time.

I remember that Jack Mossman, me, and two other culprits, whose names I have since forgotten, were playing around. Little did we know that Sister Laura, one of the shorter-tempered nuns in the hood, had quietly planted herself at the back door to take in all of our shenanigans. We had no idea how long she had stood there watching; only when she called the first name did we realize that she had caught us.

Sister Laura was short and stocky, built like a human pit bull. Her tone was ominous as she barked, "Mr. Mossman." Jack rose from his desk and took his time getting to the rear entry. He disappeared, and the waiting period began. As sweat formed on our foreheads, we pondered the perilous journey to the hallway. Who else had she seen?

Culprit number two was called out next. Jack had not, meanwhile, returned to class. Where could he be? What had happened to him? Had he been sent to the principal's office? The rectory? I'm sure the current offender thought about that as he made his way out to the corridor.

Then I heard my name. With the suspense now over, I would soon discover the fate that awaited me. As I walked out to the hall, the angry nun grabbed me by the shoulders and shook me before slapping me in the head a few times. Stunned, I thought that Rocky Marciano had disciplined me. As I composed myself, I sensed a familiarity with the technique from my compadres in crime. Obviously, the holy Sister could handle herself well at fisticuffs. I guessed that she had done the same to Jack and culprit number two before me, leaving each to wait as the next soul arrived to face her wrath.

Culprit number four was announced. This kid stood taller than all of us, including our religious version of Mike Tyson. As he walked out the back door, she took a jab at his face. Whether he had ESP or had heard the ruckus, our other sinner was prepared for the shot, and he raised his hands to deflect it.

Sister Laura shortened her swing with reflexes and skills associated only with professional boxers, counter-punching her latest victim in the stomach with her right hand. He doubled over, clearly losing his breath. It shocked him, and it surprised us, too. My imagination ran wild, picturing a Friday night at the convent where the cook burned Sister Laura's quiche. Would they put the boxing gloves on to settle the problem? Would the other Holy Sisters gather around our feisty homeroom teacher and lay down bets on who would come out on top?

Things were beginning to look up. With her last culprit now attended to, Sister Laura released her four young troublemakers before the bell, sending all guilty parties home for a lunch break. To the surprise of all of us, we ended up receiving a five-minute jump on the dismissal on the rest of the class, not a little swap for those ridiculously hard slaps and punches. The expression on the tall guy's face as we walked the long hall to our exit will remain with me forever.

The only regret I ever had was that afterward, my parents insisted on me getting my hair shortened, the cut known as a burr haircut. Whenever the nuns tried to grab my hair, they would come up empty-handed, and I would get slapped in the head or on the cheek instead. We all have our crosses to bear. To me, it was just your typical day at St. Barney's where sometimes, depending on the nun, life in the classroom was a never-ending sparring session in the boxing ring.

23

Can I Get A Ride To Wildwood?

Aunt Aggie and Uncle Vince

In the early 1960s, the Bakanauskas family bought a property in Wildwood, New Jersey, a first for anyone in our family. Positioned on Spicer Avenue between Pacific and New Jersey Avenues, its center-of-town location enabled us to walk to the best places with minimum effort. Both my aunt and uncle enjoyed the ocean. What an ideal place to let the kids loose on those hot and humid summer days! The combination of playing in the sun, splashing in the ice-cold water, and then lying in the heat would surely slow these little buggers down. Of course, they never anticipated the surge in their appetites.

Aunt Aggie and Uncle Vince treated their nephews and nieces as if we were their own and were very generous with their summer home. There was plenty to eat, lots to drink, and card games to play. My uncle had the silliest laugh when he told us his jokes. And he always laughed the loudest at his original material.

Many people may not realize the amount of work my uncle put into this house. Since he was a welder at Atlantic Richfield for many years, he insisted on rebuilding his front and back porches on all three floors using solid steel framing. He did all the rigging, fit-up, and welding himself with some help from his oldest boy, Vincy. My cousin and I often joked that those front and back decks would still be standing had the house caved in.

After graduating from high school, my friends and I got our own shore houses for the summer, often renting from my relatives. It was 1973. Since I didn't have a car, I used to hitch a ride with my uncle. His family stayed at the shore all season while he worked in Philadelphia during the week, and he would often make the two-hour drive alone, so he loved having company. And his company amused me. Riding with Uncle Vince meant listening to the Phillies game on the ride down. He and I used to talk sports all the way down to the shore. But while my uncle would never charge his favorite nephew gas money, those rides did come at a price, a cost I called *migrant labor*.

He would often have to transport an old bulky refrigerator, a gas range, or other heavy household items that he needed help to carry. Amazingly, those appliances or unwieldy objects always had to go to the top floor of the house.

The first-floor equipment operated like a finely-tuned machine; the second-level devices had little to no problems, but the third-tier household items were an absolute nightmare. I suspected that that floor was haunted and questioned whether the altitude affected the appliance operation or whether the electric power just dissipated or lost its strength. We'll never know the reason for sure, but the vital cooking and refrigeration units often failed up there. We'd climb up the steep steel steps, me praying that I'd hold my grip and not slip or fall. And those damned refrigerators weighed a ton! To this day, I lean to one side whenever I walk upstairs, and I'm guessing that lifting those bulky machines had something to do with this.

It could have been worse, though. To ride with Aunt Aggie presented a whole different set of problems. The Phillies game wouldn't be on the radio. Even worse, my aunt was a rookie driver with shaky nerves who had obtained her driver's license after turning fifty years old. Worse yet, she had a tollbooth phobia.

When I was a kid, drivers were charged tolls in both directions for crossing the Walt Whitman Bridge, and there were human toll collectors, smiling people who wished you a good day and extended their hands to take your money. Gradually, however, the process became automated, and drivers paid the 90-cent fee when entering Philadelphia from the New Jersey side.

Aunt Aggie dreaded the experience. For her to throw change and miss the exact change bucket was terrifying. Drivers approaching the tollbooth targeted the attached basket sitting conveniently to the left of the driver's window, only inches away. It was an easy toss. Yet, my aunt froze at the site, paralyzed with fear.

She would roll down her window, shut her eyes, and heave the change to her left, hoping to hit the basket. She was not accurate, not even close. Due to her panic, the money would often ricochet off the glass booth, a stray pigeon, or a car in the next lane. Quarters, nickels, and dimes would go everywhere. Soon, it seemed, four hundred vehicles were waiting in line behind Aunt Aggie's, all with drivers whose impatient horn-honking worsened my aunt's dilemma!

On Friday night, the heavy shore-bound traffic included New Jerseyans who commuted to Center City, Philadelphia, to work and who were trying to make it home for the weekend. A slew of cars backed up to the Schuylkill Expressway, a distance of five miles, with many lacking air-conditioning.

My cousin Kevin used to turn beet red as he was the youngest kid present and had to exit the automobile to pick up the change as car horns blared all around him, and people were yelling out of their windows. I would slink down the seat, embarrassed for my aunt but wishing I could put a bag over my head. I never pulled rank on my younger relative; no way would I get out of the automobile to chase down those errant nickels, dimes, and quarters.

In my aunt's defense, to lose her husband from Monday to Friday for five days a week presented her with many new and unfamiliar chores, driving a car being one of them. She had to food shop, get gas, run errands, and handle any other seashore catastrophe that might land a kid in a hospital, such as a horseshoe crab bite or a punctured eardrum from a crashing ocean wave. I was proud that she'd dared to learn this new skill at her age.

Over the years, the smiles, giggles, and pure joy of body-surfing the waves, walking the boardwalk, chasing the Fudgy Wudgy man, and riding the roller coasters became precious memories that will last a lifetime. My aunt and uncle could sleep tight, knowing that buying a shore property was the right move. In retrospect, we had wonderful times with Aunt Aggie and Uncle Vince. I still remember those rides to the shore, his car smelling like seafood because he brought live crabs for dinner on most Friday nights; hers, with its escort of honking horns and shouting drivers.

God, do I miss those two!

24

Vince At The Helm – A Night Out

Vince and Kathy Bakanauskas

In 1972, my cousin Vince worked on the Boardwalk in Wildwood, New Jersey, operating the "Satellite" thrill ride at Fun Pier. Fun Pier is the last landing on the famous wooden walkway heading toward Wildwood Crest for those who don't know. Because the prominent public attraction was always very crowded, management created measures to ensure that everyone working on the wharf was safe, including those who operated the stands where you could play various games. The Dock supervision assigned a code response to alert others if you were getting a hard time from the customers. All employees received the secret word with instructions to help their coworkers when necessary.

One hot summer night, Vince loaded the Satellite joyride with a full complement of patrons. Anyone wanting to ride needed to meet a height requirement. For insurance reasons, the operator was required to strap each rider into the compartment where they would stand for the duration of the ride, side by side in a circular pattern. The ride would spin slowly at first and then gather momentum, rapidly building speed. The spinning amusement would lift vertically about fifteen feet during its second phase before entering its third iteration. The ride tilted onto a thirty-degree angle and operated at maximum velocity during this phase. The running time for the whirling experience was ninety seconds.

This night, Vince had just started the ride when he heard the emergency code word indicating that a coworker was in distress. The altercation was close to where he worked. A helpful soul, he leaped into action, leaving his post at the Satellite to join others to assist their ally, who was operating a gaming stand and being threatened by a gang of older teenagers with whom he was having a difference of opinion. As the workers dispersed the group, outside security was already on the way to the pier. Once law enforcement arrived, they removed the problem kids from the vicinity, taking them to the local police station. Those employees who had come to the aid of their associate gathered around, feeling a sense of pride and camaraderie.

Suddenly, out of nowhere, a familiar sound startled Vince. The typical everyday background noise at a large venue like the Wildwood boardwalk included laughter, screams, bells ringing, children crying, horns blaring, and robotic-sounding voices transmitted over loudspeakers. However, the distinct note now echoing on the wind seemed distant and then somewhat closer. It was the vocal panic of people spinning in a circle and screaming for help.

Holy crap, Vince thought, *my ride's still running!* The Satellite was operating full bore three minutes later, which extended the whirling attraction far too long. The human body can spin for only a limited time before dizziness ensues.

As Vince rushed back to halt the rotating disc, people were growing increasingly frantic, some continuing to scream even as the amusement slowed, then ceased, after a harrowing 180 seconds! As Vince released the restraints that had held them in place, riders discovered that their balance hadn't exited the ride with them. Some folks walked into each other, sending bodies flying everywhere. Vince had spared no time freeing them from their captivity, but he was surrounded by a scene reminiscent of "The Walking Dead" with zombies staggering all over the enclosure in search of fresh brains. One woman nearly took a header down the steps as she exited the platform that encircled the Satellite.

Vince got lucky on this occasion considering the less litigious timeframe of the early 1970s. During this decade, people were thankful that they hadn't been hurt. Today, there would have been three lawyers calculating the pain and suffering and mental anguish that their clients had endured before the ride stopped.

If you had asked any of those customers if they had received their money's worth that night, I'm sure they would have had some strange responses. However, I doubt a single one would have asked to retake the ride. Nobody had sustained an injury or even had thrown up, which I thought most impressive. And I always laugh when I remember this story, as it could have happened only on Cousin Vince's watch.

25

The Mahogany Bureau

The treacherous Bureau

Sometimes you're lucky enough to form friendships that last forever, and it's not always with people you've known for years. My pal Jimmy Byrne is a good example. He attended St. Barney's school for only our final year, the eighth grade. I can't even tell you when we had our first conversation, but I remember that Jimmy helped me sign up for the *Little Americans* (L.A.) baseball organization. I left my neighborhood to play hardball in a league based at Myers Recreation Center, close to the parish of Most Blessed Sacrament. It was at least five blocks west and six blocks north between my home and Myers playground. Jimmy was the only person I knew.

Jim's family included eight very different characters. Jimmy was the eldest, followed by Diane, Tommy, Donald, Theresa, and John. Jimmy's dad worked at Boeing, and his job as an airplane engine mechanic kept him busy, with loads of overtime. His mom sold appliances at Silo on Lindbergh Boulevard. His parents treated me well, and the children were a lot of fun. I spent many days hanging out at their house. Jim's parents handled me like one of their kids, which brings me to the following story.

One night, Jimmy's mother asked us to come upstairs. She said she needed a favor. So we went up the staircase to the top floor, walking towards the front bedroom. She stood beside a large, mahogany bureau, an ominous-looking piece of furniture of a kind that was popular in the early 1950s. She tasked us with bringing this cumbersome antique item down the stairs and outside to the curb for pick-up. After Mrs. Byrne delivered her final instructions, she left to go to work. The trash collection for their block was the following day.

Jim and I looked at each other in dismay. The steps were long and steep, typical of the treacherous, narrow basement stairs found in houses throughout our neighborhood. So we scoped out the situation, checked the hallway width, and, once again, looked at those challenging steps. As we approached the bedroom, we noticed the ample size of the front middle window. Like two young budding engineers, we had an idea. Hey, if we managed to angle this thing just right, it might fit into the window area and save us some hauling and potential death on those stairs. Of course, we solved this problem using fourteen-year-old brains, and *why not? The bureau is being thrown out; who cares how it gets there?* We had to give our plan a try.

We moved the furniture closer to the window, and damn, we were right. It fits! We each took a deep breath, bent our knees like seasoned weightlifters, and lifted the cabinet into the frame opening at the count of three. And out it flew, crashing to the pavement below with a blood-curdling clatter. The sound of genuine mahogany striking concrete from a height of twenty feet is loud, very loud, so loud that folks blocks away wondered, *What the hell was **that?*** Babies cried, and dogs cowered terrified in their fenced-in yards, and others called 911. All the neighbors stood at their porches, wondering what in God's name was all that racket.

Having scared everyone half to death with our lame-brained idea, Jimmy and I looked at each other and decided we had better stay in the house for a while. There was no sense going outside unless the police showed up and knocked at the door. I was lucky; I had another home to go to, my own, so I wouldn't face the wrath that was surely coming Jimmy's way upon his mother's return.

Unbeknownst to us, his mother had figured that, if the bureau were left at the curb, perhaps someone else could use it. Fourteen-year-olds cannot comprehend that thought pattern. I only wished that Mrs. Byrne had expressed her intentions for the discarded cabinet while giving us her instructions. The furniture was now in many pieces scattered all over the pavement.

When Mrs. Byrne died, I was itching to tell this story at her funeral Mass, just as other folks who had loved her had offered eulogies that morning. I would have given anything to hear Jimmy's laugh echo through that impressive old Church on Third Street, with its original stained-glass windows and reverberant acoustics. He had the wildest howl. And this tale would not be disrespectful to his mother, who had a great sense of humor and who, I imagine, would have been giggling madly in her coffin.

26

A Day In Seventh Grade

We had 64 kids per class in 1967

The year was 1967. My friends and I were in seventh grade. Because we were approaching our teen years, the nuns at St. Barnabas were getting us ready for high school by allowing us to change classes during the day. We had always stayed in the same room from grades one to six while our teachers would switch locations. Now, we went to them.

Sister Marie Dorothy was my homeroom teacher, while Sister Miriam Eleanor (better known as "Pinhead") and Sister Marita John rounded out the team. We visited Pinhead and Sister Marita John twice a day for four classes, while Sister Marie Dorothy covered the rest. Sister Marie Dorothy taught Religion, Math, and Science, Sister Miriam Eleanor (Pinhead) covered Literature and Geography. Sister Marita John taught English and History. Pinhead's nickname came about since the nun's head was somewhat pointed at the top just above her habit.

Expectations differed with each woman, and each personified a specific psychological trait. The calm ocean breeze was represented by Sister Marie Dorothy's classroom manner and teaching method. *Duck before she swings* described the anxiety-laden classes taught by Sister Marita John. To round out our day, *the sitcom hour* exemplified the time spent under Sister Miriam Eleanor's tutelage; our sessions with her should have had a laugh track, like an episode of *Seinfeld*.

To explain further the differences among these Catholic servants, it's only fair to mention that Sister Marie Dorothy was young. We had a comfort level with her, and she commanded our attention. Sister Marita John was a middle-aged woman and seemed very frustrated about something in her life. Her classroom defined our first experience of undergoing stress. She could be almost sadistic in how she conducted herself, lashing out physically at boys and girls alike. Much older than the other two, Sister Miriam Eleanor appeared to have lost some of her mental faculties. She was perceived as an easy target – and that is nothing to put before sixty-five pre-teen kids under any circumstances. We should have been kinder to her because of her age.

Some of my classmates in 1967 included: Jack Mossman, Gary Bozella, Joe Courtney, and Gayle Applegate. I remember sitting for a time in the eighth row. That location carried a particular bias, and it wasn't positive. It meant that you had been pigeon-holed as evil, stupid, or both and that school authorities were betting that you'd finish your education in the public sector.

The setting for the tale I'm about to relate to was Sister Miriam Eleanor's classroom. Our Catholic education required us to behave and maintain order. At the end of each class session, we used to form a line to exit the room. One day my best friend Jack Mossman and I laughed uproariously at something I no longer recall. But it was funny because we both had our heads pointed down so that we wouldn't get caught. Within a few seconds, my partner got very quiet, his chest-heaving laugh having subsided. Suddenly, I realized that I was all alone on this one. With my head still facing the floor, my eyes fastened on what appeared to be a nun's work boot, or whatever they called those shoes. I gazed up a little at a time, slowly taking in all of the authority of Pinhead's dark, flowing robe.

When my glance reached her chin, I burst out laughing again, so out of control that she smacked me on the cheek with her red pen to bring me to my senses while the surrounding crowd looked stunned. Nonviolent by nature, Sister was angry that I had defied her. She continued to scream at me, more animated than I had ever seen her. I thought to myself, *Why can't I be like Gary Bozella,* he of the curious, high cheekbones? Gary could suck in his entire face and hold it for ten minutes, changing from the look of a laughing hyena to a mummified, blank stare within mere seconds. I so envied his skill set. Had I been that talented, I would have sustained less bruising over the years.

Suddenly, I was saved by the bell. As soon as the alarm sounded, the students, including Jack and I, marched towards the door and then out to the hallway, leaving Pinhead frantically waving her red pen around. I thought I was safe as we proceeded to Sister Marie Dorothy's room.

Later, having heard of my run-in with Pinhead, Sister Marie Dorothy pulled me aside and gave me the "I Am So Disappointed in You" speech. It always worked. Slap me around, and I wouldn't care, but mention how ashamed you were of me, and I would feel guilty for days. It's funny how psychology works, more so because she was one of the finest nuns to teach at St. Barnabas. We all liked her because her class was fun but focused. We also respected her because she brought honor and stability to our afternoon.

I made it through that year, but I must confess, it was the single most fun I ever had at St. Barney's. Nothing that happened at West Catholic High ever came close.

As I grow older and closer to Judgment Day, I know that video-tapes exist, showing me giving Pinhead problems. Picturing myself standing at the Pearly Gates, I break into a cold sweat while St. Peter loads the VCR, and a tiny nun, sporting a very pointy habit and a red pen, stands beside him saying, "Yes, that's him." No lawyer represents you at the final verdict. You are on your own.

Perhaps Jesus had a sense of humor and chuckled a few times while observing Pinhead's class and just doomed me forever to wash the heavenly pots, pans, and dishes? I can only hope that the angelic staff is kind and forgiving. Otherwise, being banished to the fires of hell will define my afterlife.

Now there's a scary thought.

27

Good Neighbors – Eva Peca

Eva Peca

We had many terrific neighbors in Southwest Philly. During the spring and summer months, we all sat on our front steps and chatted the night away. Our neighbors watched out for all the kids, too, to ensure that we didn't get into trouble.

On the opposite side across the street from us but close to Lindbergh Boulevard was the Peca household. The family included Carmen, Eva, Kathy, young Carmen, and Joseph. A big black French poodle named Gigi rounded out the group. The youngest children proved the most challenging to handle; however, this story, from 1963, is about Eva, their mother.

Eva and my mother became best friends, bonding through their jobs at the Chilton Publishing Company at 57th and Chestnut Street in West Philadelphia. To get to work from Southwest Philly, the ladies would catch the "G" bus at the corner of 62nd Street and Dicks Avenue. The PTC transport dropped them off right where they worked. But the ride could be bumpy on certain days. My mom, standing at four feet, nine inches, would never hesitate to open her mouth if something bothered her.

Unlike most other mothers I knew, Eva reminded me of the statuesque Italian starlets of the day, actresses such as Sophia Loren, Claudia Cardinale, and Monica Vitti. Eva was tall, dressed with class, and had beautiful hair that she wore up high while lounging around in Capri pants, a chic blouse, and fancy heels. Eva carried herself like a star, always looking as if she had just come from the hairdresser. Mrs. Peca also excelled with a sewing machine. Her skills as a seamstress proved invaluable to my sister Denise, who told me that Eva often took the occasion to give her tips and help her take accurate measurements for the skirt or dress she was making. No doubt that helped to make Denise the excellent quilter she is today.

One day, as Mom and Eva sat on the bus, a fellow passenger standing in the aisle gave both of them a hard time about what I never found out. Composed and mindful, Eva just let it roll off of her shoulders. However, her diminutive partner looked the guy in the eye and called him a bastard. It's always the tiny ones who have the loudest mouths – and it made Eva feel uncomfortable. This puts an unwanted burden on the taller folks now expected to protect their shorter friends. Women typically don't fight or get physical, which left poor Eva in a challenging position. Fortunately, the man stepped away. Who knows, maybe he was getting off at the next stop.

In late November of that year, President John F. Kennedy was assassinated. He was a Catholic, the first to be elected President of the United States. I was off from school that day due to illness. Upon returning, my classmates described how sad they felt at school that afternoon. I heard that most of the nuns were in tears after our principal announced President Kennedy's assassination. As a Catholic community, we were shell-shocked; so much anticipation shattered by a single bullet. It was a blow to many that left a feeling of emptiness, as if someone just poked a hole in your soul.

Eva came over to our house to watch the funeral ceremony with my mom. I remember both of them sitting on the living room couch with hankies in their hands, crying their eyes out throughout the procession. At nine years old, I realized that this was a big deal, but I didn't understand the real significance until I got older. Today when I see the tapes, the heartache amazes me.

During the horse-drawn funeral procession in Washington, DC, the television station would cut away to a proceeding in Dallas, Texas, where Lee Harvey Oswald was being escorted to a hearing. I remember the diminutive suspect being taken through a massive crowd of security, police, and newspaper reporters. The scene was claustrophobic as a mob of people crowded into a small basement hallway. Two well-dressed Federal Marshalls held Oswald by the arms directing him through the mass of onlookers. One gentleman, impeccably clad in a suit and wearing a white cowboy hat, particularly stood out. He was watching the proceedings very closely.

My mother looked at Eva and said, "They ought to shoot that son of a bitch." A minute later, a man donning a dark suit and hat emerged into camera range and fired a point-blank shot into Oswald. The wounded suspect, now barely standing, with his eyes closed and mouth agape, had clearly seen his executioner coming. Attempting to protect himself, he curled his arms tightly to his chest. In the mass hysteria that occurred, both men had let go of his arms. The surprised look on the Federal Marshall's face remains embedded in my brain to this day. His white cowboy hat, bulging eyes, and fearful stare of disbelief left a permanent impression on my psyche.

Mom and Eva sat there, mouths agape and eyes wide open. Their expressions were reminiscent of Eddie Murphy's hilarious *Saturday Night Live* take on *Mr. Roger's Neighborhood* called *Mr. Robinson's Neighborhood* when the landlord showed up to collect the rent. Although her statement was angry, my mom would never have wished for someone to be shot, and she remained shaken by this turn of events. The funeral and the hours afterward were an emotional carnival ride for her and Eva. The shooter was identified by police officers who knew him as a local nightclub owner. His name was Jack Ruby.

Like my mom, Eva left us far too soon, but she made a lasting impression on everyone who met her. I picture her relaxing at a game table, playing Canasta with all of her heavenly friends. Perhaps they've partnered up again. As I remember it, Eva would team up with Betty Zambrano to play against mom and my Aunt Barbara (mom's baby sister). The card games would last for hours as laughter and giddiness enveloped the house. And, if Eva is still taking that occasional bus ride in the sky with my mother, I'll bet that she's peeking sideways over her shoulder to make sure that the little spitfire she's sitting with doesn't cause them any problems!

28

Our Neighborhood Hero: John T. O'Donnell

Jackie O'Donnell

Although many tributes exist for our fallen soldiers these days, we seldom learn anything about them or the families they've left behind. This story is about one of these men, Jackie O'Donnell, a kid like me who grew up in the tight blue-collar community of

Southwest Philadelphia and who lost his life in Vietnam on June 12, 1968, the victim of a helicopter crash. Decades later, he continues to influence me.

The O'Donnell's lived on 61st Street between Lindbergh Boulevard and Buist Avenue. Jackie's death, felt by his close neighbors, was jarring. Folks named Carmichael, Wall, Dougherty, Giles, White, and Seamen had watched him grow from a small boy to a young man doomed to leave his beautiful tree-lined street for the harrowing jungles of Vietnam.

A thoughtful guy for his age, Jackie exuded a calm persona that made him seem much older than he was. He was the strong, silent type, quiet but hip; reminiscent of the late Hollywood movie idol James Dean in how he carried himself. For a while, Jackie dated my sister, so I spent lots of hours with him. Denise told me that Jackie always acted like a gentleman. Some nights he ate at our house because he loved my mother's Italian food. He would cut a sirloin steak one piece at a time, and I still do it that way. Why? It was an adult-like move. That was neat for a ten-year-old boy. Jackie was seventeen.

I always looked at him as someone special. He sported a beret and a black leather jacket long before they became the latest fad. He didn't smoke or drink, and he loved books, often reading to his younger sibling, Ann Marie. Jackie and his friends Jake, Denny, Ray, and Frog would sing and harmonize on the corners imitating the DooWop groups of the late 1950s. Back then, his favorite TV show was *The Avengers*, and he would always have us laughing in stitches mimicking the lines of John Steed as played by Patrick Macnee. He played sports, too. For most Southwest Philly kids, a pimple ball led to many fun games, including stickball, stepball, and boxball. One Christmas, Jackie bought me a football, and he became as close as the brother I never had.

Jackie was first reported missing. His family, including his mom and dad, his brothers Michael and Robert, and his sister Ann Marie, had to wait seven days before the military declared him killed in action. The Vietnamese had shot down the helicopter that he and his pilot, Herbert William Scott III (Bill), flew on a scouting mission. The tiny, two-passenger chopper proved challenging to locate considering the jungle terrain of Vietnam. Soldiers had to clear thick branches, bushes, and underbrush to get to the wreckage. No wonder it took a week to find their bodies.

When we received the news about Jackie, I left my family in the house to grieve while I rode my bike through the streets. It might have seemed selfish, but I needed to be alone. Perhaps I was maturing in a way myself.

Because of mom's failing health, doctors advised her not to attend Jackie's funeral. I became angry with her because she loved Jackie, even envisioning him as a future son-in-law. She communicated with him often through long, multiple-page letters that Jackie always said resembled books. I'd sent a few notes to him as well. He responded once, explaining that he and his helicopter crew functioned as a scout. Their job was to fly low and draw fire to identify and mark places where the Viet Cong foot soldiers hid. At 14 years of age, I remember telling my mother that it sounded dangerous.

Jackie's services were held at King's Funeral home on 64th Street and Dicks Avenue. I went to the wake by myself. It was my first. The line extended around the block, from the steep steps of the facility to halfway up Chelwynde Avenue. It was a long wait and a terrible time to be alone with my thoughts. Being angry at my mother for not going with me was foolish. I should have known better. She took his death very hard. A few months later, the doctors diagnosed her with Multiple Sclerosis. She died in 1973 at 44 years old, and I still carry the guilt of that anger with me.

The line snaked forward. When I arrived at the top step, containing my nerves seemed impossible. As the doors opened, the first thing I noticed was the profusion of flowers that led to Jackie's casket, stacked in multiple tiers on both sides of the aisle, and I thought to myself, *Wow, this is impressive.* The arrangements included many from the businesses and bars in the neighborhood. I suddenly realized that this funeral wasn't just for someone whom I knew but represented an entire community's coming to grips with the loss of a local soldier.

With these thoughts in my head, I looked around at the crowd in the room. Seeing Jackie's friends in tears upset me, too. There's nothing sadder than seeing the closest buddies of a young man who lost his life dazed and walking around in a fog, wondering where to turn. And if we were so touched, I cannot imagine how devastating this was to Jackie's family. He was the oldest son whose job earnings contributed to the household finances. He had two younger brothers who looked up to him and a sister who helped iron his shirts for work. When her older brother died, Ann Marie was only eleven years old.

I could now see the coffin with Jackie's picture on top and his family standing bravely beside it. They were keeping it together, and I was doing everything just to hold on. I did my best, but I broke down right in front of his mom and dad. Jackie's new girlfriend led me away to the rest area on the lower floor of the funeral parlor. The O'Donnells had to receive many more people who wanted to pay their respects. I thought that they deserved a better effort from me.

Before Jackie went to Vietnam, Otis Redding's management team posthumously released "(Sittin' On) The Dock of the Bay." Otis had completed the vocals before he died in a small plane crash, but a band member later had added a vital lead guitar part in the studio to complete the tune. Those notes, written and played by Steve Cropper, add an incredible poignancy to the tender ballad. Jackie loved it. I think of him every time I hear it. The song has such sadness to it. And the music is so coolly melancholic, appropriate to Jackie's personality.

Losing a son and a brother so young takes its toll on a household. You see it in their eyes; the glimmer is not as bright anymore. That sadness never goes away, as if someone has poked a hole into your soul. And forever, you wonder, *What if Jackie had lived?* In my heart, God made a mistake on this one. As much as He might have wanted Jackie's help, I believe that his family needed him more.

Jackie's loss was incredibly devastating. Throughout the Vietnam War, people faced that same fear whenever another call-up occurred, and more young men were drafted or whenever a son or a brother decided to enlist. Even today, as you drive around Philadelphia, you realize that every neighborhood in the city had its casualties, its survivors, and its local heroes. It is fitting and proper for us to recognize and acknowledge that.

29

Colorful Southwest Philly Lore With Jimmy

Jimmy Byrne

Jimmy Byrne was one of those guys whose heart and determination sometimes exceeded his skill set. For example, in football, Jimmy would get knocked down twice by a blocker, jump up, and somehow still make the tackle. At close to five feet, ten inches tall, Jimmy weighed a measly 135 pounds and appeared to be all arms and legs with wild, bushy hair. A gangly kid, he'd had to scratch and claw to make our high school football squad, and nothing stopped him from coming at you. Jimmy would never quit on a play. He had guts – and he was fearless.

Once, I caught a touchdown pass on the big field between 2600 Robinson and Dewey Streets. I had gotten past Jimmy and took a nicely thrown ball over my left shoulder. He stayed right on my tail as I continued to cross the goal line at the end of the park. In fact, it didn't matter that I scored; he stalked me along the rows of parked cars as if the play would never stop. As I felt his anxious breath against my neck, I thought to myself, *This crazy bastard will plow me into the concrete pavement.* As I crossed over the sidewalk just past the last bit of grass, I leaped and slid across the back of a blue sedan, hearing a thud behind me. Jimmy had stopped, but only because he'd hit the automobile in his attempt to tackle me. Meanwhile, I glided over the rear trunk, landing on my feet in the middle of the street. Talk about a close one!

Jimmy would go on to perform many daring exploits during his life. In our time at West Catholic High School, he usually rode his bicycle to school rather than take the bus. This habit continued until Jimbo woke up in a West Philly hospital one morning with a head wound suffered when he'd been hit with a brick. Because he played on the football team, like other young guys, he'd thought he was invincible.

In the 1970s, MBS parish was in a transition period. Until then, the beautiful institution had been part of the largest Catholic parish in the country. Much of the changeover was tied to economics; Northern whites were leaving the cities for the suburbs; Southern blacks were leaving rural areas for cities. Some unscrupulous realtors took advantage of the situation and chose to make a windfall through a massive housing turnover. White homeowners found notices in their doorways telling them to sell their houses while the property values were still good. This caused undue panic. And as the neighborhood changed, slowly at first, then very rapidly, friction between the resident whites and incoming blacks sometimes resulted in words escalating to violence.

We kids felt the changes, too. At West Catholic High School, former MBS students disappeared rapidly from our classes, sometimes in mid-year. Many of those students now attended suburban Catholic high schools such as Monsignor Bonner and Cardinal O'Hara. Some of our most talented athletes were gone, depleting our football and baseball teams of talent.

During our last year of play at the Myer's Recreation Center, located in the heart of MBS parish, Jimmy and I took on the additional responsibility of coaching a baseball team. The kids were ages seven to nine years. Jimmy became the manager while I worked as his assistant field coach. Jim loved working with the kids, and we stressed that all of them would get playing time. Afterward, the manager insisted on buying them water ice after every game making him their new hero. The youngsters we managed brought out excitement in us that we never saw coming. While some were raw and just learning to play, others opened our eyes with their talent and enthusiasm.

After practice, Jimmy and I routinely took a shortcut home from the baseball field. Our route took us past an orphanage between 58th and 59th Street on Kingsessing Avenue. It was our safety net since no houses were on that side of the facility. One night, by mistake, we changed our routine and walked down 58th Street.

A gang of kids followed us down the street, getting louder and bolder by the second. Jimmy and I took off running as there were at least ten of them and found ourselves trapped at the next corner on Greenway Avenue in front of a candy store. Suddenly, a creaky screen door swung open. Stepping out the door was Larry Lancaster, a fiery first baseman who played in our youth league. Standing at his front door high on the steps above us, the nine-year-old screamed at our attackers. "Hey, they're our coaches."

One of the gang said, "Larry, you know these guys?" Larry nodded yes, saving our butts. The crowd dispersed as Jimmy and I breathed a sigh of relief. Fifty years later, I wonder what became of our little hero.

After graduating from high school, Jimmy began working as a cashier at the Acme Supermarket on 54th Street and Chester Avenue near the Most Blessed Sacrament (MBS) grade school.

In 1973, the Acme store cashiers had to punch in the prices, one at a time. Scanning capability was not available then. While Jimmy rang up a customer's order, he heard an argument break out close to his lane. A young black kid was arguing with an elderly Italian man. Jimmy had several customers in line waiting for his service, but he listened to the argument escalating. He also noticed that the young dude had pulled a knife, a mean-looking switchblade.

Jimmy leaped from behind the counter and got between the two combatants without a thought for his own safety. He gripped the old man's shoulder while pushing away the belligerent would-be assailant. Amid the action, he couldn't help but notice the customers' reaction. They were staring at him in complete shock, eyes wide open, mouths agape as if to ask, *What is this crazy kid doing?* Not skipping a beat, Jimmy looked back at the customers and yelled, "More for your money at Acme!" – the exact words used for the store commercial back then. He warned the kid about using the knife. Standing his ground and showing no fear, he convinced the kid to back down and leave the store. I had to admire both his balls and his loyalty to his employer.

Sometimes it seemed that Jimmy had a knack for spotting trouble without even trying. Incidents were increasing in the supermarket, and outside on the avenue, things weren't much better. Jimmy referred to the area as a war zone.

He was working on a Friday night near Christmas when a guy strolled into the store. Wearing a large but loose winter coat, the dude walked, cartless, warily checking out his surroundings, before wandering into the meat section. There, he began stuffing packages under his shirt and into his pants. And he wasn't going for the cheap cuts. Quickly, filet mignons, sirloin, Porterhouse steaks, and loins of pork found their way into his clothes and under his coat.

The supermarket manager had recently hired a security guard to protect the establishment. While Jimmy stood at his register, he noticed the guard tracking this guy's movements. Suddenly he heard the officer shout, "Stop!"

In better shape than his nemesis, the thief made a mad dash towards the front of the store. With a quick leap, he went airborne, flying sideways at the Acme's storefront window. Resembling a linebacker throwing a football cross-body block, he bounced off the heavy plate glass, crashing to the floor. He was arrested and taken away by the police, who arrived on the scene shortly after.

(Unfortunately, on New Year's Eve that same year, the Acme was broken into. The store lost many items, including its entire meat section and, oddly enough, all the frozen dinners stored in the freezers. The store closed for good two weeks later, ending Jimmy's two years of service.)

Jimmy worked for a couple of years as a merchant seaman, making various trips to Venezuela to transport crude oil to the United States. Some of the tales he told me made me leery of ever traveling by ship. True to my fear, I never took advantage of joining the sea trials required to put a navy ship through its rigorous testing while working at the Philadelphia Naval Shipyard. One of the mechanics on the vessel passed away at sea. That night Jimmy swears he saw the dead guy's face staring at him through his porthole as he tried to get to sleep.

Although the work was exciting, Jimmy left his merchant seaman position to take a job with the Philadelphia Fire Department, eventually becoming a paramedic. He has now served twenty years in the department and still resides in Southwest Philly, close to St. Barnabas School on Buist Avenue. He remains a lifelong friend.

30

A Saint Barnabas Wedding

Jack and Denise Mossman

The year was 1974, and my best friend, Jack Mossman, was getting married. What a wedding it was! I've been to more than a few weddings in my life, but none would compare to this one.

I woke up at 6 a.m. on the Saturday of the nuptials, remembering that we had thrown a mini shindig at my house on Friday evening to finish the alcohol. We'd held the requisite bachelor party on Thursday evening. Unfortunately, plenty of liquor had remained, perhaps because two guys, one the groom, had had a minor traffic accident earlier, missing most of that event.

As I walked down the stairs, I sensed that something was wrong. I found one groomsman, Don Parkinson, otherwise known as "Park," lying face down on my living room floor. He had thrown up. I woke him up and sent him home to clean up and get some sleep. A few hours later, around 10 a.m., my phone rang. The sickly usher had a request: "Tell Moss I'm sick and can't make it."

I replied, "Park, this isn't like school; you cannot miss today. We're a team. You have a partner to walk with; you have a tuxedo; and besides, we need the procession to look symmetrical. It's bad luck to have a bridesmaid walking by herself. Take a cold shower; you'll feel better."

He made it, but honestly, the poor guy looked the sickest color of green I've ever seen.

Unfortunately, that was not the only problem that the morning presented. Next, the featured car of the ceremony, a beautiful light blue Cadillac, would not start. Curious neighbors peering from their windows to check out the proceedings witnessed several tuxedoed groomsmen pushing the automobile down Lindbergh Boulevard to get it started. If ever there existed a dark portent of things to come, this was it.

The nuptials were to be held at St. Barnabas, and I, as Best Man, did my best to make sure that Jack got over to the church early. Once we arrived, we walked into the vestibule to wait for the priest. Twenty minutes later, the celebrant entered, went to the sacristy, changed into his vestments, and announced that he was ready. I quickly peeked out the sacristy door only to discover that although all the people were seated in their proper places, the bride's family on the right, the groom's relatives on the left, the ushers weren't there.

I told the good Father that we couldn't begin the marriage service without the ushers. Just then, as if on cue but with all the finesse of a herd of cattle stampeding across a prairie, the absentees came running into the building, their new shoes clacking against the hard, shiny marble floor. Mass proceeded with nary a glitch from that point, and I thought, *Hey, things are looking up!* I should have known.

The next item on the schedule was wedding pictures. The photographer worked out of a small South Philly row house with a studio in the basement. He positioned the bride and the groom in the center, flanked on both sides by the bridesmaids. The ushers lined up behind the newlyweds and bridesmaids on a tiered set of steps.

The photographer took a few photos; then, he brought out two odd-looking chairs, each equipped with four legs, two armrests, and a piece of canvas to support the body. Neither had any backrest resembling a beach stool or hammock rather than a sturdy seat. He placed them at opposite ends of the group standing in front, and now a second portent reared its ugly head.

I was standing at the far right end of our row. My friend Bobby Cupps was on the extreme left. Although spread apart, we might as well have been joined like Siamese twins. We thought alike. Those flimsy seats might have worked on a sandy beach, but the basement floor was iffy. I gazed down the row, and from my study of physics, I knew that a potential accident was about to happen. I'm pretty sure that Bobby noticed it as well.

The woman standing on the left end, not exactly petite, wore a long-crushed velvet gown and high heels. She leaned too much to the right side of the chair as she attempted to sit down. In an instant, the scene resembled nothing so much as a spare at a bowling alley, with three women landing on their butts on the floor.

As they got to their feet and recovered their composure, we all realized that there were still serious photos to shoot, but Bobby and I had the giggles. We broke up laughing each time that the photographer asked us to pose. You know the sound when somebody is trying to stifle a laugh or hold back a sneeze, by the way, something that I could never do? Unable to get the hilarious visual out of my mind, I was in pain, attempting to control my laughter. The possibility of the photographer's presenting a professional wedding portfolio was in jeopardy. (Looking back, and not having seen that photo album in years, I imagine that Bobby's and my facial expressions made it look as if we were getting checked for a hernia.)

At a Catholic War Veterans Hall on 72nd Street on Elmwood Avenue, the reception showed Jack, a master of class, cutting the cake and spoon-feeding his new bride, Denise. However, she took a page from George Foreman's book and clocked Jack with a right cross coated with sweet stuff, practically covering his entire head with icing. I thought, *Geez Jack, are you really going to let this woman cook for you, handling sharp knives?*

After dinner, when everyone was dancing, Jack came over to me and said in an ominous tone, "Bean, be ready."

"For what?" I asked, the thought of another dark portent springing to mind.

"My in-laws love to fight," he replied.

Under my breath, I sighed, "Terrific. I can't even afford this tuxedo rental, and now we might spend the night in jail."

There was no other issue, however, and everyone went home with lives and limbs intact and, in the case of the women who'd taken a tumble, bodies only slightly the worse for wear.

As I said, what a wedding it was!

Fast-forward forty-four years. Jack has a beautiful family with three lovely girls, one boy, and many grandchildren. His son, Jimmy, is my godchild.

31

My Friend Haf

Harold (Haf) Kain

I n June of 1975, I had just completed my two-year degree in mechanical engineering technology. I was anxious to get away from all the calculations that had held me captive throughout my exam finals. So my friend Joe Kelly and I rented a summer apartment at his aunt's house on Spencer Avenue in Wildwood, New Jersey. A nice long three-week vacation filled with sun, sand, and various forms of fun and frolic was just the ticket!

Joe's brother, Mike, and sister, Denise, booked rooms as well. Mike's apartment had several rooms, so his whole gang came down. His crew included Billy Dorsch, Joe DuFrayne, and Harold Kain. Within a week of beach time, boardwalk food, and constant partying, I came to know and understand the last-mentioned name, the guy whom everyone called "Haf."

To describe Haf in a single sentence, I would have to reference one of his daily routines, which became my slogan for him: "Nothing says breakfast like an ice-cold Bud."

This hard-nosed, battle-weary Southwest Philly survivor had a tangle of long, curly, fiery red hair, reminiscent of the lion's mane, complete with its ornament of human heads, on the cover of the first Santana album. I assure you, no tailored suits from Ralph Lauren darkened Haf's closet; he typically turned out in no shirt, dungarees with a single belt hoop hosting a hanging set of keys, a prominent railroad buckle, and a stylish bandana.

The adjectives *happy, adventurous, fun-loving,* and *mischievous* would fit Haf like a custom-made suit. In his world, money was for spending, partying was the priority, and sleep was necessary only after finishing the beer keg. Every once in a while, he might even have a bite to eat, but never without his Budweiser.

In the summer of 1979, Danny Faulkner, Garry Bell, Billy Dorsch, Joe Kelly, Joe DuFrayne, Haf, and I rented a lovely seven-bedroom house in Avalon, New Jersey, on 24th Street and 1st Avenue. Haf discovered that he had no more money one particular weekend, having spent his entire three-day cash allotment on a single Friday night of drinking and debauchery. We'd planned to get some lunch on Saturday, asking Haf what he wanted. Upon checking his wallet and finding it empty, he looked at us with sad, red, pleading eyes and asked: "Did I have a good time?"

Feeling bad for Haf, we purchased a sandwich for him. After lunch, we hit the taverns, but Haf stayed home, guilt-ridden that he had spent all of his cash. While we bar-hopped, he packed up his gear and went crabbing. His method of capturing crabs comprised standing on the 21st Street Bridge and lowering a crab trap. He stuck to the basics.

Day turned into night, and we headed south to Moore's Inlet in Anglesea since the clubs in Avalon closed at 2 a.m. while the bars in Wildwood were open for another couple of hours. We had started out at 1 p.m. on Saturday afternoon but wouldn't arrive home until after 6 a.m. on Sunday morning. I would like to say that we attended Mass, but such was not the case. Believe me: most Catholic churches would undoubtedly prefer that six inebriated buddies skip the holy service.

As we entered the summer house we shared, the atmosphere reeked of something nasty and incredibly foul. It took a quick walk into the kitchen to identify the funky odor. (Before anyone gets too excited, yes, Haf was alive.) Even though the sizable home had seven full-sized bedrooms, it lacked central air-conditioning.

He had walked to the 21st Street Bridge, bringing some cold beers, a crab trap, and an additional net. He'd caught about half a dozen crabs, gotten drunk, returned home, and fallen asleep, leaving the crawling critters sitting on our spacious kitchen table. The poor little buggers had not survived the evening, lying helpless and caged in a sweltering, windowless galley. Haf slept like a newborn in his small but cozy bedroom, unaware of the mess he had created just a few feet away.

We threw the expired crustaceans into the metal trash can stored outside the building, thankful that our closest neighbor was two house-sized plots of land away from our place. The refuse didn't get collected until Monday. By then, we were all off the hook, safely tucked into our jobs at home in Philly. Some unfortunate municipal employee would have to remove that trash can lid. I daresay that after fifty hours of basting in that aluminum coffin, those crabs must have emitted a horrific odor.

Such circumstances defined life with Haf. However, the real kicker to the story is this: on that Sunday morning, at about 11 a.m., we'd heard the doorbell ring. On the porch stood three little boys who must have met Haf while he was crabbing. They asked us if Haf could come out to play. Seriously, you just can't make this stuff up!

32

Vince Takes Charge

Vince Bakanauskas

Back in the early 1970s, my cousin Vince joined our hockey team. Vince was four years younger but towered over me. We figured that he would contribute to the club just by using his size. Close to six feet tall, Vince weighed about three hundred pounds. Package that body into some hockey gear, and you have a formidable force on your hands.

As a group, we presented a small, ragged bunch of players who played with some skill but mostly with attitude. Picture a beautiful row of modern condo buildings sitting in a perfect atmosphere, now interrupted by a slew of rundown tenements. Our team represented the tenement crowd. While we weren't the most attractive team to take the ice, we brought the goods to our hockey match. I remember a game when we were missing a few players right before the initial face-off. The boys arrived late, just in time to put on their skates. After the match, we found out that they'd had a flat tire during the drive. They'd solved this problem not by putting on a spare; no, they had stolen a tire, rim and all, right off a parked car.

We played our games at the Boulevard and Tyson ice rink in lower Northeast Philly. Its shape was square rather than rectangular, a typical skating configuration of European ice rinks than the Canadian and American ice surface layouts. (Whenever they hold the Olympics in Europe, you'll see this odd-shaped arena surface.) The additional width of the international arena proved more challenging to defend, requiring talented skaters with the ability to back-check the opposing team and slow them down. In short, we needed reliable, dedicated checkers to survive.

Still feeling his way around the group, Vince knew only a few of our guys, and he was pretty young. In his first game, he skated tentatively. As a squad, we did everything in our power to keep up with the other club. But they had more speed than we did. We desperately needed a few hard checks, the kind that intimidates forwards and makes them re-think skating aggressively. Some teammates complained about Vince, "Why doesn't he hit anybody?"

Midway through the second period, it happened. Unfortunately, the smallest guy on the opposing team fell victim. The kid skated into the zone with his head down, and as Vince approached him, the diminutive winger did not sense the danger. The difference in size was astounding. Vince's shadow alone could have killed him. We heard a terrible crash, almost like a car accident. Vince not only hit the tiny right-winger, but he also drove him through the boards, or so it looked. As I glanced over, I could see Vince's body lying halfway on the ice, the other half on the bench. Under my cousin's torso, two little skates attached to two tiny legs were poking out. *Oh, Lord,* I thought, *he's dead.*

Suddenly the crowd got quiet, sensing a scary injury. I guessed that the little guy's family was in the audience, too. The opposing team's coaches were quick to help their injured winger, still lying on the bench, barely conscious. We were outsiders, so no one in the building was there to root for our guys. An angry silence was permeating through the home crowd. It's hard to describe, but you can sense the anger seeping in. First, you hear feet banging on the bleachers, then a couple taps on the glass. People start hanging out behind the nets. You continue to skate, knowing at least you are protected by a hockey helmet.

Vince had hit the kid right at the entry door to the home team's bench. Either the latch had mistakenly been left open, or Vince had destroyed the swinging entrance. Regardless of the cause, though, the kid's afternoon ended with a crushing blow. Vince was flagged with a boarding penalty. Vince shouted at the ref as he skated by saying, "Yo ref, that was a clean hit." Disagreeing, the ref screamed, "You broke the frigging bench door, and he's out cold. How the hell is that an allowable hit?" Vince, now slightly embarrassed, hung his head low and skated to the penalty box.

Just as I thought, this game was about to get dicey, the little guy stood up on his own. He looked okay but had to have been a little shaken up. I think that everyone must have let out a sigh of profound relief. And with the knowledge that the little guy was going to be all right, we began to see the absurdity of the whole thing.

None of us could get that image out of our memory. Neither our center, Tommy Bateman, nor I dared to look at each other as we would just burst into laughter. And seeing Vince out on the ice only made it worse. We weren't able to face off without cracking up and losing our composure.

Hockey is a sport of speed and balance, and a skater spends maybe a minute on the ice per shift. It's essential to maintain your temperament for skating and breathing purposes; there's no room for giggles. Unfortunately, I kept visualizing those two small skates beneath Vince's giant body. Bateman had to be thinking the same thing. We lost so much self-control that I don't even remember how badly we got beaten. Nor did I care. I now had a visual to pull up whenever I needed a big laugh. My cousin Vince and I still crack up when I mention this incident.

One of my problems as an older Catholic is to pay attention during Mass when a priest is preaching a tedious homily. My curse in life is I think of long-ago humorous incidents at the worst times. I'll be in the confessional booth or sitting in front of the boring priest when those tiny skates and legs appear again, covered by Vince. God, help me.

33

Lunch At Josephine's

My sister Denise and I

I t was 1963. My mom asked my sister to meet me at school and take me to lunch. I never understood why; it wasn't as if I'd done anything to earn this treat. At the time, Denise was in the eighth grade at St Barney's while I was in the third, and we usually walked home for our lunch, which most times consisted of a meatball sandwich, a bag of chips, and a Tastykake.

My mother worked all week while we attended class. She would make our lunches at night to save the time she needed to get dressed for work in the morning. For me, going out for lunch was a momentous event. As good as my mother's sandwiches were, getting a cheesesteak and French fries defined pure heaven to a nine-year-old.

As we entered Josephine's, on 65th Street between Buist and Elmwood Avenues, the sound of Martha and the Vandellas' "Come and Get These Memories" was playing on the jukebox. (Whenever I hear this song, it reminds me of our meal that day. Although many songs played during our break, it is incredible that I still remember this one.) Denise and I ate a cheesesteak, and we shared an order of fries.

I'm sure that some of my Southwest Philly friends must have stopped into Josephine's in the past. It served as a hangout for the older kids, too. If you're from Philly, you know that every neighborhood can boast of a slew of places to choose from for dining out. We also had an abundance of terrific sandwich shops. Hell, I didn't venture to the famous Pat's Steaks until after I'd reached the age of twenty.

As you might have guessed, a bunch of inebriated buddies and I went to Pat's after 2 a.m. Their sandwiches are okay, but Philadelphians are spoiled in this area. I laugh when visitors come to our town seeking cheesesteaks feeling that they have to go to Pat's or Geno's for a good one. They don't understand that you can get this Philadelphia staple almost anywhere in the city. And you won't be disappointed.

Back to that day at Josephine's: All the girls wore school uniforms during that period, and the boys sported a coat and tie. A few Saint Barney's kids milled about the joint, but I didn't recognize anyone. There was something unique about sitting in a booth and eating without parents present that intrigued me. It seemed as though I had accomplished some rite of passage that day as if I had achieved puberty within that half-hour.

The cheesesteaks spewed hot, melted American cheese through tasty meat that was chopped and diced just right. Our potatoes arrived blistering hot and crisp to the bite. But the best part – there was no one there to tell me to watch the salt and pepper, nobody to limit the amount of ketchup I put on the fries or decide how many napkins I could use. It gave me a sense of freedom not found when adults sat at your table. In life, you have to recognize those times you're in complete control, even if you are only nine years old.

I considered this a banner day, although I'm sure that my sister regretted having to babysit me with the constant fear that some of her friends – or worse, some guy that she liked – might show up. Spending time with your little brother is okay at home, but when you're trying to look cool in public and are stuck with a nine-year-old geek, it's a totally different ballgame that always puts the older sibling on the defensive. Whether or not Denise complained, it was the only occasion she and I had lunch together away from our house during class hours.

Though I was a handful, Denise did her best to take care of her little brother while trying to keep calm and maintain her elegant demeanor, too. We left Josephine's with full stomachs and with big smiles on our faces. We had to survive the next three hours to close out the rest of the school session, and for Denise, it was all too easy. She followed the rules. Unlike my sister, I was the kid who liked to talk, laugh, and have fun instead of behaving like most of the class. However, if I remember, I had a lay teacher that year, Ms. Connaughton, so no intimidating blue-robed nun awaited my return.

Indeed, all in all, lunch at Josephine's made for a memorable day!

34

Uncle Vince's Funeral

Uncle Vince on his boat

On May 13, 1996, we lost Uncle Vince. Although his death was not sudden, it still came as a shock. On Friday afternoon, he had experienced chest pain while carrying a case of soda up the cellar steps. The pain continued into his left arm. After about ten hours, he was driven to the emergency room at Fitzgerald-Mercy Hospital by his family. Unfortunately, the hospital wasn't equipped to perform an arteriogram, revealing any blockages in his arteries.

Instead, Uncle Vince was to be transported by helicopter to Lankenau Hospital for the procedure. Just before the flight crew arrived, my uncle suffered a Myocardial Infarction or heart attack. Although they did crack open his chest, the rupture was too large, and he couldn't be saved. The chopper pilots arrived but knew it was too late.

What a shame the timing was poor. Had Uncle Vince arrived sooner, and if the first hospital had the necessary equipment to perform the test, this perfect storm could have been avoided. Instead, we lost a proud dad, a wonderful uncle, a hard-working provider, and a funny, engaging kidder.

At sixty-nine years old, he'd still exuded energy, vitality, and a love of life. He'd worked for his entire lifetime, first welding, then performing inspections at the ARCO oil refinery for four-plus decades. To earn extra cash, he'd also fixed televisions after work and on weekends. In his free time, he'd enjoyed the things that most men appreciate – watching his favorite TV programs, including *The Jackie Gleason Show*; attending sporting events; bowling; and playing cards.

When my uncle retired, he purchased properties to repair and a boat that he kept at the New Jersey shore, where he pursued his new hobby, fishing. He and Aunt Aggie welcomed nephew Michael to their house on meatless Fridays during the Lenten season in the earlier days. Uncle Vince would bring fried seafood home from Centrella's on Woodland Avenue, sparing Aunt Aggie a night of cooking.

It was a simple life he had led, but a full one, with family, friends, and familiar pleasures. However, it is the circumstances of his funeral that make up this tale.

It's an honor to be asked to serve as a pallbearer. Rarely does anyone turn down the request. I was asked by my cousin Kathy, Uncle Vince's eldest daughter, and I accepted, and it is the cast of characters who served as pallbearers about whom this story revolves.

First, Vincy, the eldest son of Vince, walked with two horrendously bad knees due to a severe car accident. This condition caused him to hunch over like a much older man. Next was Kevin, Vincy's younger sibling. A year earlier, at age thirty-four, Kevin had had a stroke. Now recovered, he was strong, but only on the left-hand side of his body; his right torso and extremities remained stiff, affecting his ability to walk, balance, and carry any load. Kevin's desire to respect his dad was vitally important because his father had attended all of Kevin's physical therapy sessions during his long recovery.

Then came John Cassady, Uncle Vince's brother-in-law. He wore a black patch over one eye and used a cane because of a shattered leg, suffered in the crash of a small plane he had piloted. Springy (George Taninatz), Uncle Vince's lifelong friend, was otherwise healthy but 71 years old, and closing out the cast of characters was me. I have a severe foot impairment that limits my capability to support my own body weight, let alone hoist and transport heavy items.

Now some of you might have noticed that I name only five pallbearers. Kathy and I checked records, called the funeral director, and generally asked around but were able to find no one having a legitimate claim to the sixth and final spot. Given the remaining cast, I think whoever the guy was had some significant physical oddity with which to contend.

When the wake had ended and it was time to close the casket, I saw the crew of pallbearers gathered together as instructed by the funeral director. Until this point, I really hadn't known who else had been chosen for this honor. I fought down a gasp of shocked surprise and, to be honest, a feeling of sheer terror. How in the hell had the family managed to assemble a gang of guys who couldn't put one foot in front of the other, let alone hoist a hefty casket?

To make matters worse, I realized that we were at King's Funeral Home on 64th Street, right above Dicks Avenue. Anyone familiar with this place knows there are three flights of steep steps from the viewing areas down to the pavement. We had to get down these steps with a large sky-blue, bronze-trimmed metal casket containing a body. Not that Uncle Vince was a huge man, but lugging a bag of groceries was dicey enough for guys in our condition. A visual of Uncle Vince flying out of his coffin, rolling down the stairs, and crashing heavily into the parked hearse crossed my mind at least once. I thought, *Man, this could get ugly!* And prayed that somehow there would be an ambulance nearby if we needed it.

Sometimes miracles just happen. Perhaps Jesus wanted Uncle Vince in one piece for his arrival at the Big Dance. Perhaps He required some construction work or minor welding repair, or maybe Simon Peter had blown a tube on his nineteen-inch black and white (CRT) television, all jobs Uncle Vince had handled with expertise in the past. Somehow, we made it down the steps without an issue. We didn't tumble or drop the coffin, but I think I might have had my eyes closed all the way down. Thank God for the funeral parlor employees who flanked the front and back of the casket, as I'm sure that they and the Lord himself carried the load this time.

Fate wasn't finished yet, however; there was still the cemetery. The green rug that funeral directors use is a nice aesthetic touch, but it hides the condition of the boards you have to walk on to mount the casket on its bier on the metal framework around the open hole. One of the covered wooden planks shifted, rocking inward as I stepped down on it, propelling me towards the open grave. Another pallbearer caught me just as I lost my balance, and the good Lord intervened, balancing my share of the load. At least, that's my story, and I'm sticking to it because I still don't know how I managed not to fall.

For a second, I swore I heard my Uncle Vince laughing from inside his new resting place. He had a wonderful sense of humor coupled with the silliest of laughs, and I'm certain that he would have gotten a kick out of our situation.

35

The Great Rink Heist

Me warming up before our game

Back in the early 1970s, I joined my first hockey club. It started out as many neighborhood guys from Southwest Philly teaming up to learn how to play the game. We were a scrappy group that played to win, stuck together, and defended each other, making adjustments as needed. To say that we had our share of characters would be short-changing the truth.

Built in the image of the Dead End Kids from the mid-1940s, none of us boys had any money. Our uniforms didn't match. The equipment we owned was substandard. Only some of us skated well, and we had five helmets for a team that comprised fourteen players.

We played in a league whose games took place at various arenas. One Sunday morning, we were to play a game at 6:30 a.m. We drove in two to three cars, arriving in full uniform except for our skates, which we put on once we got to the locker room. We arrived at the Boulevard Pools Entertainment Complex located off Roosevelt Boulevard at Tyson Avenue in Northeast Philadelphia to discover the door open, the ice ready for action, but no one else present, at least no adult supervisor or facility manager.

I still can't imagine why a building that size would be left unwatched for anyone to walk in and wander around. Even if it was a different time and place in our history, it was still dangerous. What if someone had wandered onto the ice and fallen or walked into one of the mechanical rooms and turned off essential equipment? In today's times, and perhaps even then, the lawyers would have been climbing over each other to secure a negligence case.

One thing about playing with dudes who have no money is that they have nothing to lose. There were some wild kids in our group. Exposing these boys to an operational ice rink with no discernable supervision is equivalent to setting the inmates free in the asylum. When I looked around the clubhouse at my teammates, I pictured a future filled with detention centers, county jails, even State prisons for some. And sadly, for some, that future was realized. Others would leave us too young, like Freddie and Storky. So I wasn't very far from the truth.

Unlike some other venues, this facility featured a good-sized locker room where we could gather and discuss our game strategy. At least that's what I thought we were doing. However, it seemed that the guys had coordinated a different, more ominous plan. True to form, with no cooler heads prevailing, these geniuses decided to break into the store that shared a wall with our changing area. This retail business, known as a Pro Shop, sold hockey equipment, skates, sticks, tape, socks, jerseys, the works, and skaters could get skate blades sharpened there.

As they talked, I continued to lace up my skates. Yes, an honest-to-God scaredy-cat existed in the group. I heard attempts to break through the wall, and it didn't sound doable until they asked a sizeable teammate to help. In an instant, this larger-than-life, John Candyish-winger used his body to crush a massive hole in the drywall. It became a scavenger hunt with players feeling their way around the unlit store, like mice searching for the tastiest morsel in a dark cabinet. God only knows how much they could have taken had they found the light switch. Within minutes, stuff piled up in our locker room. First, they liberated a dozen new hockey sticks; then, someone tossed a big carton onto the floor. No one knew what the box contained, but a good shake made it sound promising. When they broke it open, a loud cheer echoed throughout the space: "Helmets!"

Ten new, shiny, white helmets spilled out of the box and onto the rubberized flooring surface meant to protect ice skate blades. What a prize this was! We could change the lines on the fly now without waiting for a faceoff. Before the heist, only five guys on our team had helmets, and as one group exited the ice, they would toss the headgear to the group coming on.

As game time approached, the guys knew they had to hide the new gear, so they put everything into the coach's car, unbeknownst to him. But anyone driving around the parking lot would have been able to spot the hockey sticks bunched up in the back seat area right next to the window.

It was still before 7 a.m., and no one who worked at the Pro Shop would arrive until at least 9 a.m., well after our game would have ended. Still, the unruly hooligans, ranging from fifteen to eighteen years old, were smart enough to know that the *Dead End Kids* needed to show up for the contest with their mismatched jerseys, beat-up hockey sticks, holey socks, and random helmets. Guiltless, we played the game, losing a close battle, three goals to two.

After the match, we informed our coach about the heist. He realized that we had to get out of there, fast. Our usual uneventful ride home had become *The Great Getaway*. He seemed angry, doubtless was, but he got it! He was a neighborhood guy, too, twenty-three years old, who was raising young children and understood the financial plight of most of these players. The following week our heretofore bedraggled bunch of skaters arrived with our spiffy new helmets, sticks, and a swagger never seen before. Amazingly, no one suspected that we'd been involved in the robbery, even though we had a fresh look and unused equipment. Someone had to have known or at least suspected what had taken place. It would not have required a degree in criminology for someone to have checked the locker room assignment and date to determine which club had dressed next to the Pro Shop that day. But nothing happened.

Looking back, as funny as this experience was on that day, we were in the wrong, regardless of our circumstances in life. I never understood why the rink personnel or Pro Shop folks didn't thoroughly investigate. We had lucked out; we all knew it, and it was a lesson learned.

As to lessons, eventually, we learned to play the game the right way. It was a fabulous and hilarious experience! I have to smile when I think of Freddie and Storky. That's where we identified with the *Dead End Kids* of the Forties. Our stories were similar to those of the Hollywood boys who lit up the big screen for many years.

Eventually, too, all of us matured and moved on with our lives, my dystopian vision largely unfulfilled. I suspect, however, that when my time comes, and I'm standing in front of St. Peter at the Pearly Gates, a large video screen will be lowered, and I will be forced to answer the hard questions.

But for now – just drop the puck!

36

A Day At The Zoo

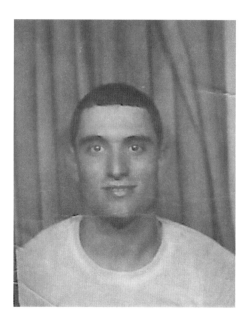

My best friend – Jack Mossman

About fifty years ago, my friend and classmate, Jack Mossman, told me a hilarious story about an embarrassing moment he experienced one day on the job. My buddy was no stranger to hard work; whether it was challenging or merely tedious, Jack was up to the task.

He'd been doing various jobs after school since the tender age of eleven, starting with stocking shelves, receiving and checking in shipped goods, taking inventory, and sweeping floors at Jim's, a grocery store in the heart of Southwest Philly. He stayed there until he graduated high school and continued to help the owner whenever he could. While still in high school, at age fifteen, Jack had had a second job on weekends, working Saturdays and Sundays at the Philadelphia Zoological Garden.

As if my classmate weren't busy enough covering his schoolwork and various jobs, Jack also had chores to do at home. While many kids in our grade school class had working parents, Jack's mom worked in Center City during the evening hours and had assigned her three children specific chores while she was at work.

Jack's younger sister, Ann-Marie, swept the living and dining room floors; Jack mopped the kitchen and bathroom, and his brother Jimmy ran the vacuum cleaner over all the rugs. Their grandmother lived with them, so the kids had someone to look after them while their mom was at her job. Jack's dad was a one-armed tile layer who worked very hard at his trade. He left home in the 1960s, and he and Jack's mother separated not long after. That's a heavy load for an active kid, but Jack proved to be a real go-getter and made the best of his circumstances.

The story Jack told me happened at his weekend post. On an early Saturday morning in July of 1971, the chief zookeeper called out sick. The boss asked Jack to perform his duties, one of which was to clean out the monkey enclosure. Jack took on this task with his usual take-charge work ethic, first lowering a ladder into the cage from the top. After he had climbed down, other crew members removed the ladder to prevent the monkeys from climbing out. That left my buddy on his own for the next hour.

Jack chose a metal shovel to remove all the leaves, scraps, and monkey waste from the floor, placing the refuse into heavy-duty steel trash cans dispersed throughout the sizable pen. As he continued to work the area, the primates hung around, taking in the new company as if it were just another day. He was surprised at how calm and accepting the animals behaved, considering that Jack had never before stepped foot into this enclosure. He finished sweeping the ground and used the scoop to place the last of the rubbish into the large containers.

That quickly, one primate grabbed onto Jack's right arm with his thin hairy arms and unyielding grip, then curled his tail onto the cage. Jack tried but couldn't move his arm at all. For a split second, he thought, *I'll whack him with the broom in my left hand.* He quickly reconsidered this idea, however, remembering what an experienced zookeeper had advised him: "Jack, never get physical with them. Have you seen the size of their teeth?"

He decided not to use his broomstick in anger, a wise choice, but a second animal latched onto his left arm, simultaneously seizing his broomstick. Things quickly went from bad to worse as a third monkey leaped onto his shoulder, totally immobilizing him.

Jack stood there, unable to move, while the other spider monkeys jumped down and flung the heavy cans all over the place. They dumped the collected refuse all throughout the cage. By now, a crowd had gathered above as Jack, still restrained by the other primates, saw all his hard work destroyed in a matter of seconds. His audience laughed hysterically as the frolicking monkeys made the poor guy look foolish. Obviously, the monkeys were breaking balls just as humans do because once the containers were empty, the animals freed Jack from their grip.

I'll never forget what he told me after this episode: "Bean, those damn spider monkeys are strong as hell. Don't let those thin bodies fool you." I was laughing so hard that I couldn't stand up. All along, I had thought that he'd been dealing with much larger monkeys, perhaps chimps or orangutans. That just screamed for someone to write a great comedy skit.

Jack was lucky that there'd been no cell phone cameras or social media or YouTube; the embarrassment would have lasted a lifetime. (Then again, he might have garnered some serious cash with the recording going viral.)

It was plain to see that Jack was not destined to be a zookeeper. Having known him from first grade, I was thrilled when he landed a job with the Philadelphia Gas Works, a career that paid terrific wages, had real benefits and allowed him to raise a family of three girls and a boy. His hard work had finally paid off, and he became one of the best at his trade.

A testament to folks who honestly put in a good day's work, Jack stayed in Southwest Philly until the summer of 1997 before venturing out to the suburbs. I count myself lucky to still be his friend over these last sixty-two years.

37

Taking Aunt Cass To New York

*Aunt Cass out front, Aunt Aggie in the middle,
and older brother Mickey in the back*

There are times in our lives when we look back with regret on things we didn't do for our loved ones. Take my mom, for example. Mom loved the sport of figure skating. As far back as I can remember, she hadn't cared for any other sports. So why did she light up during a figure skating event? Was it the music, the costumes, the elegance, the physical mastery displayed by an athlete skating alone?

I cannot answer that question because I never took the time to ask her. Unfortunately, she passed away in 1973 when I was nineteen years old. Looking back, though, I do remember her fascination with

Peggy Fleming, who was the top skater for the U.S. Olympic team in the mid-to-late 1960s, winning a gold medal in 1968. I would sit with Mom in front of our black and white TV and take in all of the frozen theatrics on The Wide World of Sports on Channel Six.

Fast forward to 1980. I met my girlfriend, Donna. Like my mom, Donna was petite and fascinated with the sport of figure skating. We attended some live events, including those that determined those skaters chosen for our Olympic team. What a difference a live event makes! As anyone who follows ice sports can tell you, these contests can be spectacular, exhilarating, and emotionally draining to view. Not only are the colors of the costumes gorgeous, contrasting with the pure unmarked white ice, but for me as a hockey player, seeing advertisement-free boards with the hockey glass removed enhanced an already eye-catching experience. We saw many future stars, including Michelle Kwan, Nancy Kerrigan, Kristi Yamaguchi, Brian Boitano, Christopher Bowman, and Paul Wylie, to name a few.

As I shared skating events with Donna, I slowly came to realize what my mom had missed. Multiple sclerosis had left her bedridden in her last three years of life. I looked back at some of those contests we attended and thought to myself, "Wow, she would have been so thrilled to witness this in person."

This realization brought me to think about my Aunt Cass, my dad's baby sister and last living sibling. She was always so much fun and also very close to my mother. But as funny and engaging as my aunt could be, at times, it was as if she carried the weight of the world on her shoulders. She was always a champion for the underdog, sometimes failing to see how she was being used. So Donna and I planned a weekend in New York City for ourselves and Aunt Cass. Our goal was to get my aunt out of her element for a fun, relaxing weekend.

The year was 2008. We booked a nice hotel and had ordered tickets to the show *Little Shop of Horrors*. We spent Saturday morning walking around Manhattan, me trying feverishly to keep Donna from going hog wild on Fifth Avenue. Although she was close to twenty years older, my aunt was still spry enough to maintain the vigorous midtown pace. We'd decided to attend a matinee performance so that we could have dinner at a reasonable hour.

As we walked into the theater, I stayed with Aunt Cass, allowing Donna and the usher to take us to our seats. As we descended the steps, I never let on how superb our tickets were. But I watched my aunt's eyes brighten and enlarge each time we passed a new row and continued down the aisle to the stage. That was worth the price of the weekend right there. Although I couldn't do that for mom, I was living it now through Aunt Cass. We were seated in Row Three. Donna and I moved into the row, giving Aunt Cass the end seat. There was a strategic reason for choosing this seat for my aunt.

The music, featuring rock 'n' roll tunes, Motown songs, even a torch song or two, echoed off the walls. Every cast member shined, with Hunter Foster in the starring role. For those who don't know, *Little Shop of Horrors* is a story about an exotic plant that feeds off people to survive. As the musical proceeds, the bush grows larger based on the number of folks it eats.

We didn't tell Aunt Cass that the twenty-foot-high shrub reaches out into the audience ten rows deep and swings both to the right and left sides of the stage. My wife knew that the houseplant would fly over her seat. It's a look I'll never forget! Aunt Cass's gleaming eyes and her enormous grin said it all.

The topper was our dinner at Da Rosina, a short walk from the theater district on Restaurant Row, about half a block past Broadway Joe's on the opposite side of the street. I ordered Shrimp Fra Diavolo; my wife, Veal Saltimbocca, while Aunt Cass decided on Chicken Parmigiana. All three of us savored our meals and concluded with dessert, a choice of cannolis or gelato.

To see the joy in my aunt's eyes that day will always lift me up. To remember her walking among the fast-moving City crowd was a testament to her zest for life and carefree attitude. Aunt Cass had invited my wife to join her in the Sephora store. According to Donna, she raved about the makeup place, saying that she had never seen anything like that before in her life.

Aunt Cass also asked Donna's advice on a Christmas gift for her goddaughter. Donna obliged, and they picked out a beautiful makeup organizer. Aunt Cass presented Donna with the new purchase when we returned to the hotel. That defined my Aunt Cass, unselfish and generous to a fault.

We lost her in May of 2018, and the world is a much less fun place these days. But now that she and mom are together, I hope she tells my mother what plans I would have had for her had she lived another thirty years. That would make me so happy! I can even see Mom's smile widen as she realizes that they remove the glass from the hockey boards when they have a figure skating event. And that it's in color.

38

Missing A Friend

Mike McGeehan

It was the last day of 2015. My buddy, Mike McGeehan, had died after a long and brave battle with cancer, a disease he had beaten once before. Despite the desire to live and see his grandchildren grow, Mike was taken anyway. "Why?" Is a question for God to answer. Hopefully, someday I'll have the courage to ask him. As for now, I get it that sometimes life just isn't fair.

Mike and I were classmates, competing athletes, altar boys, and shipyard workers who knew how to have fun and enjoy life. Although the shipyard closed in 1995, he and I had stayed in touch, mainly because we were looking for other work. I was a new engineer, and Mike was a pipefitter expanding his trade skills by learning to use AutoCAD software, a design tool used to produce blueprints for construction. I used that tool, too, and worked for a pump company near Willow Grove Air Force Base in Warrington, Pennsylvania. Some of our last emails and conversations addressed the best way to utilize this software.

I was planning to attend his funeral on January 9. And then the morning arrived, and I saw the torrential downpour from my outside deck, an unlikely occurrence in January of any year. The storm turned out to be a gamechanger. The ride to Annapolis, Maryland, would be a three-hour trip but doable armed with a GPS. At best, making that drive alone to an unfamiliar area was a risky proposition, especially given the awful visibility. I stayed home, and it haunted me.

I've heard stories that people sometimes connect with loved ones who have left this earth and had often wondered why I had never experienced this. My mom had been ill during my teens and had passed away during my nineteenth year. I'm sure that I could have used a good slap in the head sometime between my fifteenth and twentieth birthdays. Had Mom been able to reach me from heaven, she might have done it. But it never happened.

Fourteen months after Mike's death, we had gotten through the seasonal holidays of Christmas, NewYears', Martin Luther King Day, and President's Day. I was another year older and drowning in paperwork. The concentrated effort of reading the computer screen and scanning design drawings was getting the better of me. It affected my sleep. Finally, I could no longer fight off being tired. I fell into a deep but well-needed sleep – and I had a dream!

And what a dream it was. Consider: I remembered having an awful day, filled with missing orders, customer complaints, and screaming saleswomen. What the heck was going on? I didn't even work with these people. Determined to get away, I wandered around Center City Philadelphia, looking for a bite to eat. I stopped into a small sandwich spot, ordering a corned-beef sandwich on rye. The food tasted delicious, the break giving me welcome respite.

In an instant, for some unknown reason, I found myself up on the fifth floor of the old Strawbridge and Clothier Store at 8th and Market Streets. It looked very familiar. During the early 1970s, I had worked there stocking shelves in the bedspread department, my first real job out of high school.

But something was missing. Filled with nervous energy, I left the building, walking five blocks down until I reached 13th Street. I stopped and walked into Saint John's Church, spotting Mike McGeehan sitting in a pew. I had not seen him in a few years, but I was thrilled to see him today. He was dead; I knew he was, but here he was, looking bright and attentive in the first row of the church, scanning the crowd, and smiling as if he hadn't a care in the world. I took a seat next to him.

People began to arrive in droves. I imagined that Mass would start any minute, except for one minor problem: no priest showed up. Then, the front of the altar area changed, like in one of those crazy *Transformer* movies, appearing less like a church and more like a theater while a giant movie screen appeared out of nowhere. *What the hell's going on here?* I wondered. In minutes, the lights dimmed, the curtains parted, and a flick came on. It was a documentary film that covered many topics of building construction.

Hell, this was just as bad as being at work. I got up from the pew and left, temporarily forgetting I was blowing a chance to connect with a dead person who was a long-time friend dating back to the days we attended grade school.

Realization dawned. I returned and convinced Mike to come with me. He gave me an enormous smile and joined me. I couldn't get over how good he looked. He had all of his hair and was clean-shaven and neatly groomed. He smiled quickly and often. Better yet, he had that familiar laugh I recalled; a derisive *he, he, he,* accompanied by a disarming grin.

This encounter with Mike was fun. We walked up 13th Street to Market. As we passed by a loading dock area, some women dropped many plastic bottles onto the concrete floor. They rolled everywhere. Mike ran over to help the ladies sweep up the mess. I joined in as smiles and laughter surrounded us. Mike acted his jovial self again, just as I remembered him.

As we walked along Market Street, I asked Mike if he had ever experienced anxiety, knowing all he'd suffered through with his two bouts of cancer. He laughed and told me that excess stress was related to our work at the shipyard and somehow linked to our old check numbers, which we used to punch the clock. Mike and I had worked there from the 1980s through 1995. I thought to myself, how strange an answer Mike had given me. Then I wondered why I had asked that question. But what question would make sense were you allowed to rendezvous with a deceased friend or loved one?

It was at that moment I woke up. I tried to roll over and fall asleep again, hoping to continue my walk with Mike, but it wasn't happening. *Damn,* I thought, *what a shame!* I had so much more I wanted to say to him.

Honestly, I felt so good about seeing him again. He was a happy, healthy, smiling guy, just like I remembered him. The opportunity to be in his company and talk to him was a blessing I'd never seen coming. It made the rest of my morning, taking away the everyday stress of my workday.

Mike no longer had cancer. He could breathe freely without the aid of plastic tubes and oxygen tanks. I got that chance to joke and laugh once more. For that small moment in time, my friend lived again. And I know for a certainty that he meant to visit me.

39

The Life And Times Of Danny Faulkner

Garry Bell, Danny Faulkner, Karen, half shots of Billy Dorsch and me

It was only four degrees Fahrenheit when the phone rang at 5:30 a.m. on December 9, 1981. On the line was my friend Joe, who asked me if I remembered Danny Faulkner as if he had been gone from our lives for some time. Clearly struggling with how to break the news to me, Joe told me that Danny, a pal from the neighborhood and a Philadelphia police officer, had been shot at about 4 a.m. and had died at Jefferson Hospital. He was just two weeks shy of his 26th birthday.

As the story emerged, on the morning of Danny Faulkner's last day on this earth, he had been on the job and had pulled over William Cook, driving the wrong way on a one-way street in Center City. He didn't know that Cook's brother Wesley, who went by the name Mumia Abu-Jamal, was parked across the street. While Danny scuffled with William, attempting to make the arrest, Abu-Jamal, armed with a gun, ran over and shot Danny in the back. Danny managed to return fire, wounding Abu-Jamal in the chest, before falling to the ground. As he lay on the sidewalk, not able to get up, Danny rocked his body side to side to avoid the approaching gunman's fire. With intent on finishing off the young police officer, Jamal stood over Danny and fired a final bullet directly into his face. It is heartbreaking to think that such a fun-loving man, so full of life, spent his last moments staring at the barrel of a smoking gun.

To say that I was shocked would be an understatement. My first thoughts were of the cold. I couldn't imagine lying on that ice-cold pavement while struggling to stay alive.

Born and raised in Southwest Philly, Danny had had plans. He'd looked forward to what might lay ahead, to how he could further his career. Danny had enrolled in classes at the Community College, purchased a house on 6200 Harley Street, and married Maureen. He was always active, enthusiastic, and packed a lot of living into his allotted time on this earth.

He'd worked at Uncle Nick's, a local supermarket, while still in school and spent five years with the Philadelphia Police Department.

Earlier, he had enlisted in the Army and had picked up a slight southern accent while being deployed down south. This became clear when he let us hear an old cassette tape while we hung out at the shore one summer.

Danny loved to have fun playing softball but loved all sports. Dan enjoyed singing and thought we all sang well. He was wrong on that note. Most of us sounded like shrieking tomcats that couldn't have carried a tune on our backs.

In our group of friends, Danny was the organizer. He's the sole reason we never ran out of toilet paper and Irish Spring soap while sharing a place at the shore. Danny collected the money for our seasonal rentals, ensuring that even the Philadelphia Seventy-Sixers couldn't bounce our checks with all their basketball skills. He hunted and fished and loved to cook his own fish and venison. Once, in Avalon, New Jersey, he steamed shellfish on the barbecue grill, the giant clams rather than the tiny steamers. I vividly remember us guys chewing those beefy mollusks; as a result, we all achieved the jaw strength of your typical pit bull.

Danny was always the guy who would approach the saloon owner we would hang out at and seek special arrangements. He would say, "We will be spending a lot of dough here this summer; how about a bar tee shirt?" He knew that wearing those official pub shirts would get us into other bars without paying a cover charge. It was a business courtesy for taproom owners to allow competitors' workers to enter their places for free. So Danny became an entrepreneur of sorts. Plus, he was taking care of his buds.

Danny had a curious habit of just pulling off the road when he was tired of driving. It didn't matter if it was in the middle of a farm or on some small backwater town; in his eyes, he was doing the right thing and keeping it safe. Dan would typically escort home a carful of inebriated friends who would pass out during the ride, leaving him alone with his sober faculties. One night, he parked in a drive-through bank line by mistake. It became a little dicey as the township police feared we would rob the place.

Armed local cops surrounded us at sunrise when I had the misfortune to awaken before everyone else. Sound asleep in the driver's seat, Danny took a minute or two to wake up despite my pokes. Once he realized what was happening, he talked to the officers and set the story straight, and we headed home without further incident. All policemen ever want to hear is your respect and honesty. Oh, and it didn't hurt that Danny wore the badge.

On another occasion, Danny woke me up at 2:30 a.m. when I had to be at work early that morning. We rented a house near McCreesh playground on 68th Street between Greenway and Kingsessing Avenues. He was in the habit of ringing the doorbell until somebody answered. My friend Mike Kelly, who sometimes hung out at our place, was a sound sleeper. He was totally out on the couch and would not wake up. I, upstairs and tiring of hearing the chiming bells, went downstairs to address the problem.

Woozy and half awake, I opened the front door, and there stood Danny, beaming, having just returned from a hunting trip. In his arms was a freshly killed and separated deer's head lying in a cut-up Budweiser carton. It startled me, and I jumped back. Danny came in and spotted our buddy sleeping on the sofa. He winked at me and laid the animal's massive head right beside Mike's, facing him, with the tongue lolling out. After a minute, Mike awoke but didn't flinch. He burst out laughing as if this was a regular occurrence.

Danny had the kindest heart. He was the guy who would forego the biggest shore weekend of the summer to take part in a softball tournament that raised money for a local neighborhood child who was very ill. He did this several summers in a row for the little boy, who lived near 65th Street and Chester Avenue.

It would have been nice to see Danny grow old. I miss his laugh and his energy, but mostly, his friendship. Having said that, perhaps what I most regret is this: Over these far too many years, people only get to see that picture of him, stoic in his police uniform, every time an appeal comes up for his killer (who was convicted for Danny's murder in 1982 and is serving a life sentence).

For another couple of days, Danny becomes part of the news cycle again, another cop killed in the line of duty, while the folks who knew him well suffer the real impact of his loss. And in my mind and heart, that is totally unfair!

40

Sometimes Easter Isn't Ham & A Nice Suit

Harold (Haf) Kain in the headband

It was 1979 on a beautiful, sunny Easter Sunday. Our humble abode included five guys: my friend Haf, Haf's younger brother Phillip, Joe, Mike Kelly, and me. We had been renting this place for about six months now on a one-year lease. It was mid-afternoon when I heard the knock at our front door. I answered it, and a young guy, about fifteen years old, asked if Phil was home. I responded that he had gone to his mother's house for dinner. The kid said okay and thanked me. As I closed the door, it clicked. Although it was a typical sound for a door closing, something seemed out of sync.

Like a trigger, the sound was followed by an explosion that knocked me against the living room wall. Upstairs, a piece of the bathroom skylight had fallen onto Haf while he was washing up to go out for the night. He staggered down the stairs, pressing a towel to his bleeding head. I called 9-1-1 and reported to the police that someone had bombed our property.

Going outside to check, we saw the house to our immediate left in flames. A mother, three kids, and three dogs lived there. Haf and I ran in to get the children out, but they weren't there. Neither were the two larger animals. But the mom was standing in the living room, oblivious to us and screaming for her puppy. Our luck, or lack thereof, the pup was upstairs.

Without thinking, Haf leaped onto the staircase, ran up to search, and found the little critter in the main bedroom. By now, the fire engines had arrived. The chief asked if everyone was outside. We told him that the place was clear, and he instructed that we were not to go back inside. With smoke and water damage, it would be hours before we could enter the building.

What had happened was that a home two doors away had had a natural gas explosion. Lying face down on the lawn was the steel front door, still encased in brick, along with three attached concrete steps. Later, we discovered an eight-foot diameter hole at the back of the house, enabling us to see the kitchen area. Thank God, no one had been there. Meanwhile, our other neighbor's residence continued to burn with the raging fire.

Southwest Philly, being blessed with multiple barroom options, we chose Bob's Grill at 68th Street and Chester Avenue. Only a block away, it had three things we needed; beer, entertainment, and a bathroom. Not able to help or enter our place, we walked to the corner saloon.

As the night wore on, we continued to drink. Haf, feeling his oats, was talking to other customers at the taproom. The puppy rescue tale took on a life of its own, going from a sweet, brief story to a full-fledged novel. In the latest edition, Haf had the staircase engulfed in flames, requiring him to cover his face, leap over furniture, and slay a dragon to get to the small doggy in the front room. His listener looked on with amazement, eyes getting wider by the moment with Haf's much-exaggerated version of saving the tiny pup. In reality, Haf had scurried up a fire-free stairway and found the canine sitting in the middle of the master bedroom. But those who knew Haf well understood that he was apt to embroider his tales given his colorful existence.

We were able to reenter our place at around 1 a.m. on Easter Monday. All the fire engines and equipment had left the scene. My Navy Yard shift would begin at 7:30 a.m. As I scaled the stairs to my tiny, second-floor bedroom, the thought of sleep proved more than usually inviting, as my intake of beer had mellowed me.

I found my door slightly ajar with the lights off in the darkened hall. I pushed it open, sensing that something was amiss, but not yet within reach of the light switch. In that instant, a sizeable object ran between my legs, scaring the living hell out of me. From what I surmised when I regained my wits, one of our neighbor's bigger dogs had panicked, taken off out of that property, and found his way into our home, where he'd taken refuge under my bed. Thank God I was a young guy back then, or this might have been my last Easter.

Inevitably my 9-1-1 call resulted in an interview with a police detective. My mention of a firebomb required me to answer a few questions concerning any problems we might have had with the neighborhood teens. In reality, the home devastated by the blast had been vacant for months. The people who lived there also owned a warm-weather cottage to which they retreated each winter.

We learned that some kids had broken into the empty house to steal the copper piping. One nitwit had disconnected the natural gas line, allowing the volatile vapor to accumulate throughout the two floors of space. Another guy came along later with a lit cigarette in his mouth and happened to poke his head inside the basement window. I never found out if the explosion had injured him.

Both the intense flames and high-velocity streams of water poured on them had damaged our next-door neighbor's place so much so that it wound up being demolished within the month, leaving a sizeable gap between our property and the one that had exploded.

And as my pals and I had discovered, sometimes Easter isn't just ham and a nice suit!

41

Whew, That Was Close

Fuji

Back in 1980, I had my tonsils removed. At twenty-six years of age, I went through the surgery wide awake and under a local anesthetic. The nurses sat me in a chair similar to what you would find in a dentist's office and blindfolded me. I wondered, "What the hell did I get myself into here?"

During the procedure, the surgeon and his assistants had a good old time at my expense, but I surmised that the nature of this episode was to relax me. And it did. However, that line about getting ice cream after the operation is only accurate for the little ones. Apparently, older folks have issues with bleeding, which is why they put you in a seated position. For me, I had a whale of a sore throat and did not eat for eight days except for a bowl of chicken Pastina soup on the eighth day.

I was single, so my sister Denise volunteered to take care of me. I stayed on her couch for that entire week as she waited on me like big sisters do. But I'd rented a place in Avalon, New Jersey, for the summer, and I wanted to escape and breathe some refreshing ocean air.

I left for the shore that Friday morning, arriving just after noon. This season, I shared a tiny home with freckled Joe, Billy, Joe Kelly, and Haf (Harold Kain). When I settled in, I found out that another buddy had stopped by. He had arrived with a cold case of beer, and our house rules dictated that he could stay. His name was Fuji, nicknamed after Mount Fujiyama.

Already a big guy, Fuji had an unusual trait in that his physical size seemed to expand relative to the amount of alcohol he drank. One afternoon on the dance floor at Jack's Place, part of this distinct change occurred at 36th Street and Ocean Drive, where Fuji showed off his moves. Magically, like an ice hockey fighter in his prime, he would find extra space opening up all around him. We used to call his style of dancing the Monster Mash because he was all arms and legs. Had you been there to witness this phenomenon, you would see the live band backing up farther onto the stage, fearing Fuji's reach. Sometimes the club managers tolerated this, and sometimes they directed the bouncers to toss your butt out of the bar.

This was one of the latter times. The day was not working out well for Fuji. The doormen showed him the way out of Jack's Place very early into the afternoon. Smart enough not to drink and drive his car, he was now faced with a two-mile walk back to our house.

Meanwhile, I rested comfortably in a bedroom that contained a couple of single beds, oblivious to all of this. After sleeping for an hour, another guest arrived. She was the "baby sister" of a friend who had stopped to see the gang. At twenty-one, she wasn't exactly a kid, though we all protected her as we would a little sister because she was five years younger than we were.

I was the only guy home at this point. I'm sure that my snoring led her to check the back room. She sat down on the other single bed to talk to me. As I was describing my lousy week, we heard a thunderous crash. Our galley was right next to the bedroom where we were talking. Apparently, someone had walked through the kitchen door and had an accident.

Before we could react, Fuji reached our doorway and poked his head through the opening. Looking like a caveman, he spotted the girl and grunted an unrecognizable word. Our female guest, suspecting imminent danger, announced, "I'm with him!" and jumped into my bed.

All I could think at the moment was, *Oh my god, I've eaten one small bowl of chicken Pastina soup in the last eight days, and now I might have to hit this big son of a bitch.* That quickly, Fuji staggered into the room, collapsing against the wall, falling onto the other mattress while ripping down the window blinds simultaneously. He was out cold! *There is a savior*, I thought. Then I turned to her and said, "Do you realize that he could have kicked both of our asses with no problem?" (Folks, this wasn't cowardice, just a reasonable assumption from a starving, emaciated, tonsil surgery survivor.)

Fuji slept it off and didn't remember what had occurred. From my perspective, he might have been joking all along, but that loud crash was not the back door being opened. Fuji had fallen over the kitchen table, knocking several items to the floor before scrambling to his feet and appearing in the bedroom doorway.

As long as I'd known him, Fuji had never exhibited a violent tendency that I remember (although we did hear reports from our neighbors that a clumsy, linebacker-sized man had been seen punching Stop signs on the way home from Jack's Place that day). Until then, Fuji had been just another enthusiastic, uncoordinated guy at the disco. He wasn't alone. Only Joe Kelly could muster up some legitimate dance moves among the guys in our household, but he had many sisters, so he always got some extra practice at the family castle. We did have some dudes who pretended to dance, but TV star Deney Terrio's *Dance Fever* job was safe and secure from us.

If I could have told Fuji anything to be learned from that episode, though, it would have been, don't drink and get larger; it's dangerous for your health and well-being.

42

Heaven Snares A Goalie

Mike Nolan (Noz)

One Saturday in April of 2017, I received a call informing me that one of our goalies had died. Mike Nolan, or as we called him, "Noz," hadn't started out goaltending but had switched after playing defense over some years. I remember him as a steady defenseman who played physically and led his team. If you needed a big hit to change the momentum, Mike delivered it. Mike would score if goals were scarce at a crucial moment in the game. He was also a vocal leader, always talking the guys up and keeping them loose. Mike could carry the puck out of the zone and play the blue line with finesse. Why did he switch to net-minding? I never found out. And it never occurred to me to ask him that question because his on-ice presence never changed. You knew he was a straight shooter, no bullshit.

Mike's personality lit up in every locker room that he entered. The kind of character who keeps everyone loose, Mike exuded humor and was quick to smile and laugh, but he specialized in breaking balls. If a hockey fight broke out, Mike jumped in. Think of Philadelphia goalie Ron Hextall going after Montreal defenseman Chris Chelios right after the talented blue-liner delivered a cheap hit against Flyer's winger Brian Propp. His intensity and take-charge attitude will give you a sense of what made Mike special because most goalies avoid the fighting.

When we won the championship that year, Mike led the team to a midnight swim in a lake in Maryland. Our popular winger, Joe, had invited us down to his Eastern Shore house for a party. Drinking and late-night swimming do not pair well! (Perhaps I should also mention that no teammate wore trunks into the frigid water.)

I remember riding to a game in Radnor, Pennsylvania, in mid-afternoon, approaching rush hour. Sproul Road, which runs between St. Peter and Paul Cemetery and Cardinal O'Hara High School, was icy and snow-covered. I was a passenger in Joe's Jeep, along with Mike and a few other guys. We were already running late for the contest as the vehicles slowed to a crawl.

After twenty minutes of snarled traffic, we picked up speed. The treacherous roadway had severe ice patches, and we hit one. We were sliding sideways, perpendicular to the street, and continued to do so for another 150 feet. How we made it through that experience without having an accident is something that only God knows. We had no clue. But someone was watching over us because the team did well in the playoffs that year.

As the years went by, we continued to play together in the various men's leagues, but Mike left Philadelphia in 1980, moving to Cape May County to be closer to his job as a chef at the Avalon Country Club. Living at the Jersey Shore meant that he had to travel a long distance to our games. On most game days, Mike arrived with goalie equipment and a bag of edible goodies. He had little time to get his hockey gear on. After the contest, we would change into street clothes and out came the food. Mike brought sandwiches with him and distributed them to the team.

In 2016, I spent considerable time with Mike at Burrs on the Beach, an annual event for West Catholic High School graduates. He had been ill with cancer for quite some time and had had to have part of his left arm amputated at the elbow. Did this stop Mike? No! Instead, he had fitted a sock over his stump and demonstrated his artistic skill by drawing Donald Trump's face on it. Mike displayed his unquenchable spirit throughout the day by entertaining everyone using it as a puppet gag. He joked about losing one of his significant defensive assets, his goalie glove hand. That was Mike – taking what others might have seen as a tragic situation and turning it into live entertainment.

Mike smiled all day long, thrilled to see some of his Southwest Philly neighbors and teammates. I didn't realize this was the last time I would see my friend, which makes me very sad. Mike's final impression was much like everything he did in life. He told me that he had further medical appointments at the University of Penn and was ready to fight his disease.

I can't imagine sitting in his shoes, knowing that he had to undergo more treatments while walking with a crutch and minus half an arm. But Mike had never feared anyone or anything and approached this cancer battle as he would have another hockey opponent: "Come anywhere near me and be ready for my best because I'm bringing my A-game."

I realize that no one is guaranteed a carefree existence, but why do the good ones get sick? It's a cruel joke to take a character away that lived each day to the fullest as Mike did. I can only guess that Heaven needed a great goalie and someone who could stand in for a defenseman, too. You know, a guy who also made delicious sandwiches, drew fantastic pictures, and always kept the crowd laughing – a guy like Mike.

I'll never forget the last time I saw him. His joking manner, bright smile, and rosy cheeks hid any fear he might have had about his time left on earth. It was as if he was telling us that all would be fine, and he was happy and content with the knowledge that he meant so much to everyone and had made such a lasting impression on teammates and opponents alike.

Rest in peace, my friend, and save me a seat on whatever bench you're on!

43

Honoring A Classmate & Teammate

Joseph Courtney

Joe Courtney was one of a kind. Tall, with close-cropped hair and a freckled, smiling face, I remember him from the first days of attending St. Barnabas School. One morning in second grade, Joe and his buddy Freddy, both bigger and more imposing guys, tossed me about the coat closet. They roared in laughter as my tiny body got tangled in all the coats, with their accumulated particles of dust and lint. I recall Joe calling me Snotnose 38. Okay, so I couldn't breathe through my nose. I still can't.

A bundle of laughs, Joe would be our live entertainment in class. He always told a joke or created a scene that made everyone laugh. Surrounded by those intimidating nuns while reciting multiplication tables and reading catechism passages hardly amounted to an exhilarating day. Our classmate would change all of that.

Joe was the only guy who could keep Sister Marita John laughing. It was an uncanny skill on his part. He also tapped into something no one else foresaw. Our English & History teacher must have secretly loved baseball because Joe convinced her into playing the Phillies games on the radio during our afternoon session. What a pleasant break on a warm spring day! She would always laugh at his jokes, even the silly ones. It was hard not to like Joe.

Once, during our seventh-grade English class, Joe's efforts backfired. Our homework assignment was to diagram a rather complex sentence and present it to the teacher. We all lined up with our copybooks in hand to show how well we had done. If the structure was laid out correctly, identifying the subject, verb, object, prepositions, adjectives, adverbs, and any pronouns, you returned to your seat with a smile on your face. If you botched the exercise, the good Sister would take your copybook and slap you in the forehead with it. Both guys and girls endured this curious penalty. On this day, she seemed determined to take no prisoners.

I remember that Joe sat in the last row in her room. Sitting there in a Catholic school usually signified that you presented a challenge: you were some kind of problem child, likely headed for a public institution. Anyway, when Joe's turn came, he jokingly referred to the difficulty of our diagramming task to the nun. She didn't chuckle. After viewing his solution to the project, the unpredictable woman did something different. Instead of hitting Joe with his thin notebook, she chose the three-pound history textbook and clobbered him with that. You could hear the hush throughout the classroom. Everyone was surprised; no one more than Joe.

As much fun as he was as a classmate, he became an even better teammate. I enjoyed playing St. Barney's football and Millick Street baseball with Joe. He played catcher for our neighborhood club. Always a great competitor and a talented athlete, his nickname at the time was Cookie. Although Cookie Rojas was a popular Phillies player, that wasn't why Joe had that nickname. I never knew why they called him Cookie. Maybe he ate all the chocolate chip cookies at home?

While playing center field at Finnegan's playground, I made a costly error, causing two runs to score for the opposition in the fourth inning. It was now the seventh inning, and we were still behind by three runs. We faced our first loss of the season as Joe came to the plate. Joe hit a shot over the right fielder's head with the bases loaded. This miracle line drive morphed into a grand slam as he cleared all three bags and scored the fourth run for us. With a walk-off homer, the entire team mobbed Joe immediately. Boy, had he saved my bacon! I felt so appreciative of that. As a group, we remained undefeated until our last contest, the City of Philadelphia's title game, which we lost by a score of 1-0.

For as playful as he could be, Joe was a down-to-earth kind of guy, too. I've always remembered the day when he fought a kid who was a grade ahead of our class. That was rare in those days, but Joe's taller stature made him appear older than the rest of us. The senior boy had challenged Joe. After school, the fight occurred on one of the side streets between Buist and Elmwood Avenues at 64th Street. Joe boxed smartly and held his own. I gave him the win because the other youth bled all over his white, nicely pressed, long-sleeved shirt. But as true sportsmanlike competitors, Joe and his opponent both shook hands at the end of the fisticuffs.

I've had brief communication with Joe over the years from time to time. The last time I saw him was at our grade school get-together back in 1993. That night he laughed with the gang, that boisterous laughter that we all recalled so well. Though Joe and I hadn't talked recently, I mentioned him on my visit to see Sister Marie Dorothy this past May. The nun told me he was a handsome boy. She remembered his picture when I showed her our reunion booklet.

Joe died on November 1, 2017. I will never forget Joe for his impact on me, even in the most insignificant moments. Folks say that you affect a person's life more than you'll ever know, so you must treat people with respect because it makes a difference. It is true. Joe and I had that respect. Just thinking about Joe will always bring a smile to my face. Rest in Peace, my friend.

44

Spending Quality Time

My dad, Mickey McCullough

I've been thinking a lot about my dad lately. His name was Michael, but everyone called him Mickey. He was raised in the Grays Ferry section of South Philadelphia at 2600 Titan Street. My father was five feet seven inches tall, with broad shoulders and beautiful blue eyes, the eldest of four children, who included sisters Aggie and Cass and little brother Johnny. Dad left high school after completing 10th grade and found himself in the Navy within a few years. I'll never know how he got there because he was underage.

He also had a rare skin disorder on his feet that made walking or standing exceedingly difficult and running almost impossible. It severely limited the kind of jobs he could do. How this got past the military in the first place is anybody's guess, but once the Navy found out about my dad's feet, they honorably discharged him. Mickey decided to drive a cab, working for The Yellow Cab Company.

During this time, he met a tiny Italian girl named Margie. After a couple of years together, they eloped, getting married in Elkton, Maryland, in 1949. They moved into a home on a tiny street called Sears Street, near 36th and Wharton. Close to their property sat the Grays Ferry Avenue Bridge, where Southwest Philly folks traveled to reach many parts of South Philly. Mom and dad went in the opposite direction, leaving Grays Ferry to buy a house in this new area called Southwest Philadelphia around 1956. The big draw was that the more recent homes had decent-sized back yards and front yards, too.

Although mom died in 1973, dad stayed in the neighborhood until 1998, living near 72nd Street and Lindbergh Boulevard in an apartment complex called Unico Village. It was here when Dad started to develop dementia.

Three days before Christmas in 1998, dad suffered a mini-stroke in front of St. Irenaeus Church, only a minute from the court where his first-floor apartment was located. Because of his dementia, he no longer recognized the entry gate and instead stood there, getting soaked in a downpour of rain. Oddly enough, he was in his pajamas, too. But Mickey had the luck of the Irish because the temperature that December day had reached 73 degrees. I point out his good fortune because we received four inches of snow the following day. Our temperature dropped from 73 degrees to 32 degrees within twenty-four hours!

On that day, we knew that my father could never live alone again. After he was hospitalized for the stroke, followed by a short stay in a nursing home facility, my sister and I were able to get him into an excellent assisted living home in New Jersey, close to both of us. He did well there for his final three years of life, dying at the tender age of 73.

In the last few days of 2017, I viewed the film *How the West Was Won*, an epic western tale released in 1963. From the second it started, I was reminded of my father. He had taken me to see this motion picture many years ago when it was showing at the President Theater on Snyder Avenue in South Philly. My dad loved all flicks but reserved a special place in his heart for Westerns.

Unlike him, I had tired of the Western movies, in no small part because many television shows during the late 1960s featured cowboys and ranchers. I remember *Rawhide*, *Bonanza*, *Have Gun Will Travel*, and *Gunsmoke*. However, this epic movie was one of only two films shot using the Cinerama process, a wide-screen method to project images from three synchronized 35 mm projectors onto a gigantic, curved screen. This new system existed only in theaters.

Fifty years later, when I discovered that I could purchase the motion picture on Blu-Ray at a low price, I had to give it another viewing, mainly because of my memories. Spectacular, eye-opening effects defined the presentation on my sixty-inch HDTV television. The colors, contrasts, and the sheer magnitude of the scenery were breathtaking. A robbery scene set on a train looked every bit as realistic and tense as what you would expect from today's newest technology. The screaming locomotive looked to be leaving the tracks at any moment. Meanwhile, gunfire and screeching brakes upped the ante as cowboys and thieves battled for control of the train. I found myself ducking out of the way on my own couch.

High-Definition Television and Blu-Ray movie discs were invented a few years after my dad died. I only wish my father could be with me now to see this film, transferred from its master tape to Blu-Ray. He would have loved the viewing experience accompanied by the 5.1 Surround-Sound scores. Dad was used to stereo but never heard music separated over more than two speakers.

There were other great movie experiences with my dad, too. He would take me to the President Theater on the weekends. It was there that we viewed *El Cid*, *The Man Who Shot Liberty Valance*, *In Like Flint*, and *Dr. No*, the first James Bond film. Sometimes, my parents would pile us kids into their automobile during the summer for one of those fabulous dollar-a-carload nights at the 61st Street Drive-In. With movies, Dad was all in. He focused on the plot, paying complete attention to the script. His enthusiasm enabled me to appreciate the artistry of making films. It's a feeling I still have to this day. As a result, I've collected a library of motion pictures that I watch over and over. I never tire of them.

Even at nine years of age, when my father took me to the theater in South Philly, I developed my first female crushes while watching these films. Whether my dad realized that is something I'll never know, but I appreciated it all the same. For example, Sophia Loren starred in *El Cid*. She was one of the most beautiful actresses ever to appear on the silver screen. Ursula Andress played a part in *Dr. No.* with Sean

Connery. Her scene emerging from the water wearing a white-belted bikini with underwater goggles was iconic not only for the fashion industry but for the actress herself. It made her a star.

As my father aged, I would take him to our local theater on the weekends. We saw *Saving Private Ryan, Meet the Fockers,* and a few others. If we didn't go out to a movie, I would rent flicks from a nearby Blockbuster store or pick a few from my collection. He and I would sit for hours, taking in as many pictures as possible. We ended our day either at a nice restaurant or at our home, where I would cook steaks, burgers, shrimp, or crab cakes. And we had to have dessert. Life just isn't complete without a sweet treat. If he stayed with us overnight, I would always prepare a hearty breakfast for him.

When I was younger, he and I both worked different shifts for most of our lives. We developed a strong bond over his last difficult years while spending many hours together. Even though he no longer had a short-term memory, just sitting there with him, laughing, discussing a plot, and talking about the old neighborhood were moments well spent. It was the true meaning of *quality time*. I only hope he got out of it what I did. I sure miss him! And I've long since forgiven him for always knowing who the killer was before anyone else knew.

45

The Bakanauskas Pool Party

Front: Aunt Aggie and Uncle Vince,
Middle: Anne, Monica, and Kathy. Back: Kevin and Vince.

You haven't lived until you've been part of a Bakanauskas Pool Party. I would define this event as pure wet mayhem driven by breaking the rules, causing scenes, and living out your everyday acrobatic nightmare. Think of the scene in *Caddyshack* where the caddies arrive and take over the entire public swimming pool.

My Aunt Agnes, formerly a McCullough, married a tall, handsome Lithuanian man named Vince Bakanauskas, and the rest, as they say, is history. The couple would have five children: in order of age, Kathy, Vincy, Kevin, Anne, and Monica. However, only the boys will play a part in this drama set at my sister's house, at a graduation party for my niece Megan, who had just graduated from high school.

My sister has a nice-size in-ground pool in her backyard. Most kids spent that day swimming and playing around, taking a break only to have a hot dog or hamburger. The group included children from both the Irish and Italian sides of the family and those wild Lithuanians.

As a kid, my cousin Vince had constantly terrorized pool attendants who worked at the various motels and hotels found along the streets of Wildwood, New Jersey. Back in the 1960s, these pools had lifeguards assigned to watch after their guests. They were very strict that non-paying customers could not use their facility. Vince would randomly jump into a pool and take the occasional dip on our three-block walk from home to the beach. Just diving in would drive those rescuers crazy. This meant nothing to Vince, who swam like a dolphin and stayed out of their reach. He was agile despite his size.

Now, twenty-five years later, we take this same attitude into a family pool party. Vince, now the mature dad, instructed his children to stay in the shallow part of the pool. As Vince yelled at his firstborn son and namesake to remain in the safer area, the little guy held onto the side of the structure, slithering further into the deeper end while looking into his father's eyes. Needless to say, this was in total defiance of his pop's wishes. Suddenly, off in the clouds, I could hear the ghosts of the Wildwood lifeguard's past, laughing like demonic clowns.

As the celebration moved into the evening hours, the sun went down, and a fresh breeze filled the air. My cousin Kevin, Vince's younger brother, wanted to show off his impressive diving skills. At six feet four inches tall and 250 pounds, he's not your typical diminutive gymnast. The springboard design dictated diving off where the water was ten feet deep. A sloped wall existed two-thirds of the way from the diving board to transition to the shallow area.

Kevin did his best Johnny Weissmuller impersonation and took a long run out to the edge of the board, getting a great spring with his dive. I looked to my left, and I swear he was halfway across the length of the pool before he broke the plane of the water. No sooner had Kevin done so than we all knew what was coming: my cousin would crash into that sloped wall. And he did. Hard!

Vince immediately dove in and got his brother to the surface. Kevin's diving form had been correct. His arms and hands had been out in front of him. But his momentum and the impact of hitting the barrier were against him, and he compressed his neck. Having worked in research and development labs for a considerable period of his life, Vince realized that he needed to restrain his brother's head and neck. When the ambulance arrived, the paramedics praised him for safely securing Kevin's upper torso, particularly his skull and vital stem. They rushed Kevin to the Kennedy Emergency Room in Washington Township, a short ten-minute drive away.

I volunteered to go to the hospital to assist Kevin's girlfriend and relay the news to the family. Really, there was no one else to do it. My sister hosted the party, where seventy-five people were still hanging around. It was a weekend, and I knew that it would be a long night filled with the typical weekend injuries, and indeed, we were there for about three hours.

Thankfully, Kevin was not seriously injured. The medical facility released him that evening, his tail firmly curled between his legs, but otherwise okay. If this drama were to have a lesson, it would be that one does not simply take Southwest Philadelphia folks out of Philly and plant them at poolside in New Jersey.

I would be remiss not to mention the safety precautions for all future Bakanauskas pool parties: 1) remove the diving board; 2) place the elderly folks far away from the water; 3) have paramedics on duty just in case. With safety checks completed, happy swimming!

46

Margie's Little Angels—Dot Bateman

Dot dancing with her son, Tommy

From 1967 on, mom, diagnosed with multiple sclerosis, got through each day with some helpers. In the early stages of her disease, people would show up at our house to do what they call "patterning." This is a process where four individuals gather around the hospital bed and work your arms and legs in patterns similar to stretching, walking, and lifting. It helps the muscles to keep moving as multiple sclerosis patients sometimes lose their mobility. Left unworked, muscles and tendons will atrophy and eventually become useless.

Besides bodily help, the brain requires stimulation. With everyone in the house otherwise occupied, it can be a lonely experience, especially for someone as active as my mother had been throughout her life. She loved talking, singing, dancing, cooking, cleaning, and throwing shoes at me. While I was in grade school, she worked at Chilton Publishing Company, counting on my older sister Denise to monitor me until she got home. Mom continued to work until it became unsafe for her to walk. By this time, I was a sophomore at West Catholic High School.

Dot Bateman was a neighbor who lived up the street from us. Her husband, Ted, worked for the railroad. Teddy, the eldest sibling, was closest to leaving the nest, headed into the Army serving in Vietnam. Bobby, the middle son, was in high school as I was. The youngest, Tommy, was three years younger than me. Dot had her hands full caring for these guys; however, this never prevented her from dropping by to cheer my mom up. Dot, by nature, a funny person, would tell tales that would have Mom in stitches for hours.

Dot worked at the Penn Fruit Supermarket, which bordered the vast parking lot across from G.C. Murphy's on Woodland Avenue. Much like my mom, though, she always seemed to have a tan. She spent a lot of time out in the sun. In those days, the women hung the clothes on the clothesline in the backyard to dry. Her husband was a hard-working guy, too.

Teddy and Tommy were excellent athletes. They were guys who were talented enough to play ball for a living. Bobby, the middle boy, had his brothers' speed but nowhere near the skill and coordination associated with being a natural athlete.

As might be expected, most of Dot's stories reflected the daily issues she had with her clan, which were entertaining as hell. For example, Mr. Bateman had this awful habit of waking up in the middle of the night and screaming for help. He wouldn't get out of bed. He would just sit up and yell "Help!" at the top of his lungs. (I had first-hand experience hearing this once on Christmas Eve when I stopped in for a visit. Whether it was nightmares, fear of the dark, or just lousy coffee, she never told me the reason for these episodes.) Dot was sitting across from me in her favorite chair beneath a beautiful Japanese painting, watching a holiday movie on the television. Both Bobby and Tommy came downstairs to join us, comfortable in their robes and slippers. Suddenly, Mr. Bateman let out a yell, and Dot just sat there and rolled her eyes as only she could.

On another Christmas Eve, Dot revealed this tidbit. Unfortunately, Mr. Bateman became ill and fought cancer for some years, eventually learning that it was terminal. With this information, Dot and Ted decided to purchase a family plot for the burial. They brought along sons Bobby and Tommy for the meeting with the undertaker. Bobby was not thrilled, but he managed. However, by the time they got to Tommy, the poor little guy was spooked and took off. I can't say I blame him; funeral parlors scare me, too. But Dot's telling of the story had me practically rolling on the floor. Her imitation of the sound of Mr. Bateman yelling for Tommy was hysterical.

When my mother passed away on September 16, 1973, both Dot and her son, Tommy, came down to comfort my family and me. To this day, I remember what a beautiful Sunday morning it was as we sat on our front steps and talked. It was well-known that my mom had been confined to a bed for a long time on our street, so other neighbors stopped by to express their condolences. Both Dot and Tommy hung around for most of the day, which was a big help to us as our family started to visit as well.

Before my sister Denise got married in 1969, our house was a popular stop for my sister and her friends since my mom loved having them over so they could play the popular tunes of the day. It made her much lonelier when Denise got hitched, and it really saddened me to see mom trapped in that bed and not able to get around.

After her husband died, Dot lived for a few years in the Wildwood Villas. I wanted to visit her in her home in the Villas, but I never got there. She died when I worked in the private industry for a pump company in Warrington, Pennsylvania, sometime between 1996 and 2000.

I was in my first engineering position out of college, one that required a one-hundred-mile daily commute from New Jersey. Too new to the profession, I couldn't get time off to attend Dot's funeral, as she was not a family member. That was a shame because it would not have been a problem had I worked for the federal government.

Dot was undoubtedly one of my mom's special angels. I have no doubt that her place in Heaven is assured. I will never forget her sense of humor and her wonderful laugh. Such a kind and caring person as Dot Bateman should wear her halo proudly.

47

Leaving Southwest Philadelphia

Our wedding day

I left my home in Southwest Philly in December of 1989, having purchased a brand-new property in South Jersey. Donna and I had married that month and were eager to begin our lives together. The move would require that both of us drive our cars to work or to the nearest available public transportation. Donna decided that her best choice was to travel to Center City Philadelphia via the PATCO (Port Authority Transportation Company) High-Speed Line, a good decision because parking in the city was limited, not to mention expensive.

Gone was her ability to walk around the corner from her home in Fishtown to board the El train at the Girard Avenue station into Center City. My commute to the Philadelphia Naval Shipyard was a thirty- to forty-five-minute trip traveling on Route 55 North to Route 42 North, where I crossed the Walt Whitman Bridge, exiting at Broad Street to the shipyard.

I sold my home to a good friend who lived with me at the property for close to five years. His parents had moved out of the Most Blessed Sacrament parish to Delaware County. His goal was to become a Philadelphia Police officer, which required him to live in the city.

This New Jersey living was all new to us. We now had an assigned parking space to use with plenty of spots on our lot that were first come, first served. I no longer feared coming home from work during a snowstorm and getting stuck having to park on the bus route street because my street had no spots available.

In Southwest Philadelphia, I found myself limited to parking on 62nd Street, where in winter, because of bus traffic, snowplows would come through overnight and bury my car under mounds of snow. Not only would I have to dig out of the spot to get to work, but when I returned home after my eight-hour shift, that space would be taken. Sometimes I felt as if I was the only person on my street who had a job.

Looking back, one of the main reasons I moved out of Southwest Philadelphia was because of my car insurance premiums. The purchase of a new Hyundai Excel saw my insurance climb to two-thousand dollars a year. I called my insurance company and questioned the rate, as my new vehicle was tiny and efficient on gas mileage. I was told that because I lived near the used auto-part places on 61st Street, there was a risk that my car would be stolen and used for parts. Apparently, they considered some auto-part businesses "chop shops," where cars are stolen and broken down to sell the pieces. In New Jersey, insurance for both of our vehicles amounted to one-thousand dollars.

After relocating to New Jersey, some differences were immediate. Unless you lived in a new development, there were no sidewalks. We have several parks where built-in trails for those who walk to exercise. On the negative side, people jog in the street with no regard for automobile traffic. You must drive everywhere; no one walks to any store.

In Southwest Philly, we had corner stores almost everywhere that sold lunch meats and cheeses, bread and rolls, canned goods, dairy products, cereals, bathroom products, newspapers, and cigarettes. Although New Jersey has the Wawa and Heritage stores, which sell all of the staples, ask anyone from the Southwest Philadelphia Catholic parishes about the term, "Put it on the bill." You won't find that happening in any New Jersey stores. Store owners in Southwest Philadelphia felt sorry for those with large families and allowed them to build up a tab that the parents would resolve after payday.

While New Jersey has plenty of organized sports programs, including baseball, football, and soccer, try to find kids playing in the streets. Not only do there seem to be fewer kids, but you also don't see them outside often. Southwest Philadelphia had all the ballfields in the world between Finnegan's, McCreesh's, and Myer's playgrounds, but our streets were filled with kids playing stepball, wireball, baseball, and football. We dove behind cars, cut around telephone poles, jumped over trash cans, anything to further our skills for playing sports.

After living in New Jersey for over thirty years now, I still haven't seen a fireplug being used unless it's for fighting a building or house fire. As kids in southwest Philly, we spent hours staying cool under the fireplug, which ran under full pressure at city and taxpayer expense.

On Halloween, we Southwest Philadelphia kids traveled all over the neighborhood, going door to door and carrying multiple bags or pillowcases for our candy. Nobody bought Halloween outfits in those days. Some of the old folks used to ask us to do tricks or play games, sometimes guessing who we were behind the costumes. And we went out in the evening, after dark, not at 3 p.m. because it wasn't safe. Over the last ten years in New Jersey, we've had fewer than fifteen kids ring our doorbell. The previous two years, no kids at all came to our door. And this is a lovely area.

Maybe the most unfortunate and saddest change is the decline of the Catholic churches. In southwest Philly, seven parishes vied to serve our families: Saint Barnabas, Saint Clement, Saint Irenaeus, Our Lady of Czestochowa, Good Shepherd, Our Lady of Loreto, and Most Blessed Sacrament. All of these churches had elementary schools associated with them. Saint Barnabas had grades one through eight, with three classes per grade totaling 1,400 kids. Most Blessed Sacrament was even more significant with, in its peak years, eight classrooms for each grade, with approximately 3,500 kids.

All schoolchildren were required to attend Mass each week. Each class was responsible for going to religious services at a set time on Sundays. The children's Mass at Saint Barnabas was always at 9 a.m. Even though some Catholic schools exist in New Jersey, children's attendance at church is sparse at best. There are CCD (Confraternity of Christian Doctrine) classes for children who want to learn about the Catholic religion.

Maybe it's a sign of the times but living in Southwest Philly gave me many friendships in my life, some dating back to first grade. For me, that's keeping the same buddies throughout sixty years. I'm not alone; my wife, from Fishtown, near Center City, Philadelphia, still has many friends from her youth who stay in touch. Is this accidental? I don't think so. Because we attended Catholic schools, we were together for close to twelve – formative – years.

When you think of the number of kids that went to school with you over all of those years, it's incredible how many friends you have. Couple that with your close neighbors in southwest Philly. Row homes are conducive to making friends or enemies. Frankly, you are practically on top of each other, but that puts you into situations where neighbors can help each other.

Many folks came from South Philly to buy the newer homes that would become Southwest Philly. I remember people walking freely into their neighbors' houses to chat, borrow some butter, or bring donuts. That trait followed along with our neighborhood. A simple knock on the door followed by a hello was all that was required. Try that move in New Jersey; it's simply not happening. In fact, it is considered rude to ever stop at someone's home without calling first.

The Washington Township neighborhood where I live today is beautiful. The homes are kept exquisitely, and the landscaping can be breathtaking. Houses come in many sizes and shapes, based mainly on individual developers. But something is missing. People don't hang out outdoors and make friends easily for all of the beauty you see. We live in a condominium building with eight properties, four (two-story) units on top of four (single-story) units below. While we've made some friends throughout the years, there are very few we would call close friends. And that seems to be the knock-on New Jersey.

Once a year, I attend a high school reunion in Wildwood, New Jersey, for all classes that went to West Catholic High School. Sometimes as many as three thousand folks show up for this six-hour school fundraiser. I love seeing the people each year. Once I ran into a gentleman who graduated in 1933. I graduated in 1972. We talked and hit it off immediately. More impressive, though, is that many old Southwest Philly residents attend the affair, and it's as if we never left the neighborhood. Laughter ensues for the rest of the event as we talk about our upbringing, including the old stickball games and the rough-touch football in the big park.

We were raised to respect our elders and call them either Mr. or Mrs., never by their first name. I still do it that way; it's automatic. We knew that our neighbors were watching us because so many of our parents had to work. We all looked out for each other and always were encouraged to help out when we could. To ask an elderly neighbor if they needed anything at the grocery store or if we could shovel their sidewalk and steps was encouraged by our parents, and that's how you build a community. Caring for one another pays dividends; it really does.

To a person, my friends and I all agree that we had it made in those days. All the building blocks were already in place. From our parents to the neighbors, to the religious orders of nuns and priests over the years who guided us as young men and women, to an abundance of volunteer coaches who taught us how to play sports the right way, to so many kids to play with – what more could a kid ask for? It was like we found our own heaven on earth! Our memories tell us that we are correct! I can't imagine growing up anywhere else or any other way.

The End